The New

Enchantment of America

MICHIGAN

By Allan Carpenter

 CHILDRENS PRESS, CHICAGO

ACKNOWLEDGMENTS

For assistance in the preparation of the revised edition, the author thanks:

KAREN A. HART, Travel Bureau, Department of Commerce; MICHIGAN BELL TELEPHONE COMPANY, for the commissioned paintings of Robert Thom in the Series "A History of Michigan in Paintings."

American Airlines—Anne Vitaliano, Director of Public Relations; *Capitol Historical Society*, Washington, D. C.; *Newberry Library*, Chicago, Dr. Lawrence Towner, Director; *Northwestern University Library*, Evanston, Illinois; *United Airlines*—John P. Grember, Manager of Special Promotions; Joseph P. Hopkins, Manager, News Bureau.

UNITED STATES GOVERNMENT AGENCIES: *Department of Agriculture*—Robert Hailstock, Jr., Photography Division, Office of Communication; Donald C. Schuhart, Information Division, Soil Conservation Service. *Army*—Doran Topolosky, Public Affairs Office, Chief of Engineers, Corps of Engineers. *Department of Interior*—Louis Churchville, Director of Communications; EROS Space Program—Phillis Wiepking, Community Affairs; Charles Withington, Geologist; Mrs. Ruth Herbert, Information Specialist; Bureau of Reclamation; National Park Service—Fred Bell and the individual sites; Fish and Wildlife Service—Bob Hines, Public Affairs Office. *Library of Congress*—Dr. Alan Fern, Director of the Department of Research; Sara Wallace, Director of Publications; Dr. Walter W. Ristow, Chief, Geography and Map Division; Herbert Sandborn, Exhibits Officer. *National Archives*—Dr. James B. Rhoads, Archivist of the United States; Albert Meisel, Assistant Archivist for Educational Programs; David Eggenberger, Publications Director; Bill Leary, Still Picture Reference; James Moore, Audio-Visual Archives. *United States Postal Service*—Herb Harris, Stamps Division.

For assistance in the preparation of the first edition, the author thanks:

William C. Todd, Tourist and Convention Service, Henry Ford Museum and Greenfield Village; Michigan State Library, Lansing; Lynn B. Bartlett, Superintendent, Department of Public Instruction, Lansing; Willard C. Wichers, Director, The Netherlands Museum, Holland; Lewis Beeson, Executive Secretary, Michigan Historical Commission; Henry J. Ponitz, Chief, Adult Education, Department of Public Instruction, Lansing; Michigan Department of State; Automotive Section, Detroit Public Library; Community Relations Department, Ford Motor Company.

Illustrations on the preceding pages:
Cover photograph: Mackinac Island, James R. Rowan
Page 1: Commemorative stamps of historic interest
Page 2-3: Michigan Dirt Road in Autumn, Travel Bureau, Michigan Department of Commerce
Page 3: (Map) USDI Geological Survey
Pages 4-5: Detroit Area, EROS Space Photo, USDI Geological Survey, EROS Data Center

Project Editor, Revised Edition:
Joan Downing
Assistant Editor, Revised Edition:
Mary Reidy

Library of Congress Cataloging in Publication Data

Carpenter, John Allan, 1917-
Michigan.

(His The New enchantment of America)
SUMMARY: Traces the history of the state with an account of the formation of the land, the people, the utilization of natural resources, and the expansion of its industries.
1. Michigan—Juvenile literature.
[1. Michigan] I. Title.
F566.3.C3 1978 977.4 78-8001
ISBN 0-516-04122-3

Contents

A True Story to Set the Scene

IN THE NAME OF THE KING

A wooden cross lay on the bank of a river. Beside it was a cedar post, carrying a shield with the crest of King Louis the Fourteenth of France. Below rushed one of the mightiest rapids in the world. And all around for hundreds of miles stretched the wilderness.

Seated around the cross and the shield on the slope of the river bank was a great crowd of Indians from fourteen different tribes. They were strangely silent, waiting for something to happen. For months they had been hearing about the wonderful things they would see on this day, the fourteenth of June, 1671. They were there at the invitation of their friends, the French priests who had just built a mission near the rapids.

At last the door of the mission opened, and a procession came out. Leading the procession were four missionaries in their black robes. Following them strode a dramatic figure unlike any the Indians had ever seen, wearing the handsome uniform of an officer of the French king. After him came his attendants, interpreters, and many French hunters and trappers, all wearing bright-colored sashes and other decorative accessories that would make them look more impressive to the Indians.

The solemn procession halted before the cross. As it was being planted in the ground, the great cross was blessed. Next the pole with the shield was raised with a chant and a prayer for the king. The officer stepped forward while guns were fired, drew his sword, and slashed a piece of sod from the earth. Holding the sod aloft in one hand and his raised sword in the other, in a loud voice he claimed for his king all the land to the ocean of the north, to the ocean of the west and to the ocean of the south. He repeated this three times, while his followers shouted, "Long live the king!" and fired their muskets in unison.

Opposite: The Pageant of the Sault *depicts François Daumont claiming most of North America in the name of the French king.*

1966 Michigan Bell Telephone Co., Robert Thom

The officer was Francois Daumont, who is generally known by his title, Sieur de St. Lusson. He had been sent by the French governor of Canada to make a formal claim to most of the North American continent in the name of the king of France. To make the act seem even more official, St. Lusson asked the priests and other Europeans to witness and sign a report that the land was now officially French.

One of the missionaries, Father Allouez, next made a speech about the power of the king. "When he attacks, he is more terrible than the thunder; the air and the sea are set on fire by the discharges of his cannon. . . ." At the end of the speech the Indians shouted in amazement. They "were all astonished to hear that there was any man on earth so great, rich, and powerful."

The Indians could not know then that they had just seen the Pageant of the Sault, the start of events which would lead to the loss of their beloved hunting grounds.

This event, which took place on the banks of the St. Marys River where Sault Ste. Marie stands today, is only one of the many early stories of the enchantment of Michigan.

Catching Whitefish on the Sioux, *a painting by George Catlin.*

Lay of the Land

WATER WONDERLAND

Many people fear that some day there will not be enough fresh water for everyone in the United States, and many states and cities will begin to suffer for lack of water. If that day ever comes, Michigan will certainly be a favored state. For Michigan really is, as one of its slogans goes, a "water wonderland."

In an Indian language that was once spoken in Michigan, *michi* means "great" or "large." *Gama* is the word for "lake." So the name of Michigan itself comes from Indian words meaning "great lake." Michigan can truly claim to be the land of the Great Lakes, since no other state has as much shoreline on the Great Lakes. Of the five Great Lakes, only Lake Ontario fails to wash the state's shores.

The lakes also divide Michigan into two p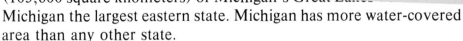sula and the Lower Peninsula. It is the only that has two parts completely separated in s

Michigan is the largest state east of the M holds this record only because of its great a eastern states have more land than Michigan (147,686 square kilometers), but adding alm (103,600 square kilometers) of Michigan's G Michigan the largest eastern state. Michigan has more water-covered area than any other state.

The two square miles (five square kilometers) of water for every three square miles (nearly eight square kilometers) of land give Michigan the greatest proportion of fresh water to land of any similar land area in the world.

It seems strange indeed that an inland state, far from any ocean coast, should have more shoreline than any of the states with long ocean coastlines, but Michigan once had the longest shoreline of all the states. It was only when Alaska became a state that Michigan's coastline of 3,121 miles (5,022 kilometers) lost its first-place rank and dropped to second.

In addition to the Great Lakes, Michigan has more than 11,000 inland lakes, many of them of good size. No place in Michigan is more than 85 miles (nearly 137 kilometers) from a Great Lake or more than a few minutes by automobile from some lake.

The four Great Lakes nearly surrounding Michigan also help to make the state's climate warmer in winter and cooler in summer than that of other states at similar north latitudes.

Michigan also has many rivers. The Detroit River, the St. Marys River, and the St. Clair River (which, because they connect two large bodies of water, are really straits) are among the most important waterways in the world. They connect the three upper Great Lakes with the St. Lawrence River and finally with the ocean. Some of the many true Michigan rivers are the Tahquamenon, Saginaw, Grand, Black, and St. Joseph.

Many things about the geography of Michigan are surprising. Port Huron, Michigan, is as far east as Greenville, South Carolina. It is farther from Detroit to Houghton, still in the state of Michigan, than it is from Detroit to Baltimore in the "far-off" state of Maryland.

Britain, Sweden, and Belgium are closer to Detroit by water than is New York City. And, strangely enough, a portion of Canada lies to the south of most of Michigan, although we think of Canada as our neighbor to the north.

BEFORE HUMAN MEMORY

Michigan's land was not always like it is today. Both sandstone and limestone are found in Michigan. Sandstone comes from the packed sand of ancient beaches around ancient seas. Limestone comes from the crushing and packing together of the shells of dead animals of the ocean. Because sandstone and limestone are found where oceans have once been, experts in geology believe that Michigan must have been at the bottom of a shallow ocean at one time, and possibly several times, as the oceans came and went millions of years ago.

Much later Michigan was almost entirely covered by water again, but this time it was the frozen water of the glaciers during the ice

View of Eagle Harbor lighthouse
on the shoreline of Lake Superior.

ages. Several times the sheets of ice pushed over what is now Michigan, bringing with them rich soil from Canada and great rocks and boulders. As the ice melted, it left behind valleys and hollow places carved out of the land. Many of these hollow places became lakes. Even the Great Lakes were formed in this way.

A few areas still to be seen in Michigan today were not changed by the seas or glaciers. One of the most interesting places anywhere is the region near Houghton, in the Upper Peninsula. The copper-bearing rocks there are believed to be among the oldest rock formations in all the world, apparently having existed there practically without change almost from the beginning of time.

13

Footsteps on the Land

THEY NEVER WERE SEEN

Before Europeans came to Michigan, there were no written records of the people who lived there. However, we know there were many different people who occupied this region. They left many things that tell us something about them and the way they lived, but we really know very little about their daily life. We have found a few of the mounds they made as burial places for their dead or for other purposes. Some of their ancient implements and weapons have also been discovered.

Not as many of these reminders of ancient peoples are found in Michigan as in some of the nearby states. Some of the most interesting traces left by prehistoric people are found on Isle Royale, an island in Lake Superior. There, ten thousand copper-mining pits worked by prehistoric peoples have been found. We can only guess from this that some of the early peoples were skilled enough to work with copper at about the same time the ancient people of Egypt and the Sudan began to fashion the same metal in their far-off desert land.

By the time Europeans had arrived in Michigan territory, the people there were different from those who had been expert enough to work copper. For some reason the native people of Michigan in the seventeenth century were working exclusively with stone implements.

SNOWSHOES AND CANOES

When Europeans came to what is now Michigan, they found Chippewa (sometimes called Ojibway), Ottawa, Potawatomi, Miami, and

Opposite top: Indians on Snowshoes, *a painting by George Catlin. Opposite bottom: Ottawa Indians spring planting, from a diorama at the University of Michigan Exhibit Museum.*

Menominee Indian tribes living in various parts of Michigan. Later the Huron (or Wyandot) group came. Wars and changing food supply kept the Indians on the move, so that the various tribes occupied many different areas at different times in history.

The fierce Iroquois Indians had driven almost all the other Indians out of the Lower Peninsula of Michigan, and for years this was practically a "no-man's land." When the Europeans came, they also avoided the Iroquois, and the first settlements were in the far-off Upper Peninsula, as far away from the Iroquois as possible.

The Indians made two great contributions to the European explorers. Without the Indians' snowshoes, it was impossible to travel overland in the heavy Michigan snows, and their bark canoes have been called the "cleverest small craft ever devised."

The Indians hated their enemies, but although they were much misunderstood by the Europeans, they were loyal to their friends. It was the coming of the foreigners that caused their downfall.

UNDER FOUR FLAGS

The first Europeans to reach what is now Michigan came from the older French settlements along the St. Lawrence River. They were still looking for a way to cross the American continent and reach the Pacific Ocean, where they thought they would find the Orient and all its riches. It is generally agreed that Etienne Brulé and his companion, Grenoble, were the first Europeans to touch Michigan's soil. They are thought to have reached Michigan sometime between 1618 and 1622, and at about the same time they discovered the largest of the Great Lakes—Lake Superior.

Another young French explorer who was searching for China was Jean Nicolet. The French governor of Canada was so sure Nicolet would reach China that he gave him a beautiful silk robe, decorated with heavy gold braid and jewels, so that he would be suitably dressed to meet the emperor of China. Nicolet probably made his way through the Straits of Mackinac in about 1634 and may have reached as far into the interior as Green Bay in Wisconsin. Although his gorgeous robes were very impressive to the Indians, he was disappointed in not reaching the Orient.

Other French explorers, fur traders, and Roman Catholic missionaries began to reach the upper Michigan country. In 1641, two Jesuit missionaries, Fathers Isaac Jogues and Charles Raymbault, gave the name *Sault de Sainte Marie* to the rapids in the river that flows between Lakes Superior and Huron, and it has been called the Sault (or Soo) ever since.

The very first permanent white settlement not only in Michigan but in all the Midwest was made at the Soo. The settlement was founded in 1668 by the famous Jesuit missionary Father Jacques Marquette and his companion Father Claude Dablon. It was here three years later that the Pageant of the Sault took place, with France claiming most of North America as her own territory.

Although Europeans had been in upper Michigan for many years, it was not until 1669 that any European visited the Lower Peninsula. Adrien Jolliet, older brother of the famous explorer Louis Jolliet, is thought to have been the first European to go into the lower part of Michigan.

Most of the early French in Michigan were fur traders and missionaries. Some of these expert French woodsmen were called *coureurs de bois,* or trappers, and others *voyageurs,* or boatmen. The traders were successful in buying great quantities of valuable furs from the Indians, and the missionaries converted a number of the Indians to the Christian religion.

But not many French people came as settlers to occupy and farm France's New World territories. In 1689 there were only twenty thousand people in all of the French colonies of North America. Although most of the English settlers were found along the Atlantic Coast, in that year there were already more than three hundred thousand of them in North America.

Alarmed at the growing power of the British, the French began to build forts. Father Marquette and Jolliet left St. Ignace on an exploration trip in 1673. Marquette died near present-day Ludington in 1675. In 1679 the famous French explorer La Salle built the first French fort in lower Michigan on the site of what is now St. Joseph.

Sieur De La Salle and the Griffon, *St. Ignace, August 27, 1679.*

He called it Fort Miami, after an Indian tribe in the area, and it became a thriving military and trading post.

In order to transport furs to market, La Salle built the first large boat to sail on the Great Lakes. It was called the *Griffon.* Loaded with furs, the *Griffon* set sail one day in 1679 and was never heard from again. What happened to the *Griffon* and its cargo is one of the many mysteries of the Great Lakes.

In 1686 Daniel Greysolon built Fort St. Joseph at the site of present-day Port Huron. By 1700 the French had become more disturbed than ever about the British, who were competing for the fur trade in territories the French claimed as their own. In 1701 a French officer founded a town between Lake Huron and Lake Erie, at a spot where the water runs through a narrow strait. He named it with the French word for strait—*Detroit*. Detroit is the oldest of all the major cities of the Midwest.

One of the famous names in America is that of the French officer who founded Detroit. But most people know his name not because of his success in establishing a great American city but because in that same city more than two hundred years later his name was given to an automobile. Today we see the name of the founder of Detroit, Antoine de la Mothe Cadillac, on most streets in the United States.

Soon after Detroit was founded, Madam Cadillac and Madame Tonty, the wife of Cadillac's assistant, made the long and hard journey from France to join their husbands in Detroit. They became the first European women in Michigan. Cadillac had brought 150 persons to Detroit and by his firm and fair treatment he gained the respect of the Indians who were living there.

Because many French leaders were afraid of his power and were jealous of him, Cadillac was forced to leave Detroit in 1711, but he was given the post of governor of the faraway Louisiana Territory.

Still disturbed by the threat of the British, the French set up Fort Michilimackinac on the Straits of Mackinac in 1715.

During the years that followed, the French and the British were sometimes at war, sometimes at peace. At last, however, in the war we call the French and Indian War the British were successful. Major Robert Rogers and two hundred of his Royal English Rangers occupied Detroit in 1760, without a struggle. French rule of Michigan was almost at an end.

The French settlers accepted the British rule without much complaint, but before long the English were having many difficulties with the Indians. The French had treated the Indians as their friends. They often invited them to be guests in their homes, and many marriages of French men and Indian women took place.

The British, however, considered the Indians inferior, and generally treated them with little regard.

An important Indian chief, Pontiac, resented the British and decided to organize a movement to drive them out. He planned to capture Detroit by a trick. He had the barrels of his guns trimmed off so they could be carried under the blankets the Indians wore. Then he asked to speak to the British commander at Detroit and brought his warriors into the fort with their concealed weapons. The commander, Major Gladwin, had been warned, and he had so many soldiers armed and ready that Pontiac decided against trying to carry out his plan.

Later, in 1763, Pontiac attacked the fort at Detroit and began the longest siege in the history of Indian warfare. For 175 days the Indians tried to capture Detroit. At the beginning Major Gladwin had only one hundred soldiers and twenty merchants to hold off the hundreds of Indians, but Pontiac was never able to take Detroit.

Detroit, however, was the only fort in Michigan that did not fall to the Indians. This was the period of the Indians' greatest success in their struggle against the Europeans.

Another group of Indians used a different trick to capture the fort at Mackinac. The Indians started to play a game of lacrosse outside

Fort Mackinac, *by Seth Eastman*

This diorama at Mackinac Island State Park shows the Chippewa uprising at Fort Michilimackinac on June 2, 1763.

the fort. The British soldiers came outside to watch, leaving the gates open. They paid little attention to the Indian women who strolled inside the fort, but they carried knives and other arms under their blankets. On a signal, the Indians left their game, hurried into the fort where they received arms from the women already inside, and then massacred the defenders.

Later, in spite of his victories, Pontiac finally was forced to make peace, and the British again gained control of Michigan.

But their control was not to go unchallenged for very long. The Americans began their revolution against Britain in 1776. Very little direct effect of the Revolution was felt in Michigan. But the British commander at Detroit, Lieutenant Governor Henry Hamilton, became one of the most hated men in American history for his part in the American Revolution.

Hamilton was called the "Hair Buyer," because he offered the Indians money for American scalps. He felt this would help to destroy American settlements.

During the Revolution, in 1781, one of the strange happenings in Michigan history was the raid of a Spanish party from the Spanish lands west of the Mississippi. The raiding party reached the fort at Niles, in southwestern Michigan. They captured and held it for several days. This was the only spot in Michigan where the Spanish flag ever flew, but it can be truthfully said that four flags have flown over Michigan—French, British, Spanish, and American.

AMERICAN OR NOT?

When the Revolution was over, the Treaty of Paris of 1783 gave Michigan to the Americans. In spite of this, the British stayed in Michigan for another thirteen years, and the Americans were not strong enough to do anything about it. The British were determined to protect their rich fur trade in the region as long as possible.

After many defeats by the Indians, who were receiving much help and encouragement from the British, the Americans finally sent a famous Revolutionary War hero to capture the western lands. This was General Anthony Wayne, who was called "Mad Anthony Wayne" because he took such "mad" risks during the Revolution.

With brilliant and careful planning and preparation, General Wayne was successful, and the Jay Treaty of 1794 finally gave the United States the right to occupy her lands in Michigan.

General Wayne himself traveled to Detroit in August of 1796, and the whole town turned out to welcome him in one of the most joyful celebrations the city has ever known. The name of "The Chief Who Never Sleeps," as the Indians called him, has been given to a city, a county, a university, a fort, and a museum—all in Michigan and all named "Wayne."

Today, with the exception of some names and memories, there is very little evidence remaining of the long rule of the French and the shorter rule of the British in Michigan.

Even before Michigan came under American rule, the young country had set up plans for governing it. The Northwest Ordinance of 1787 established the Northwest Territory, which included the present-day states of Ohio, Indiana, Illinois, Wisconsin, part of Minnesota, and Michigan.

The Northwest Ordinance was one of the great statutes of history. It set the whole pattern for the growth of the United States. Instead of being governed as colonies, the western lands were to be given the opportunity to become states with all the privileges of the original thirteen states. If some other plan had been tried in the Northwest Territory, the United States might have been quite different.

Michigan remained a part of the Northwest Territory until 1800, when it was placed in what was known as Indiana Territory. In 1805, Michigan became a separate territory, with Detroit as its capital, although not all of present-day Michigan was included in this territory.

When the Michigan Territory was created, for the first time the settlers in Michigan were going to have at least a small voice in their own government. President Thomas Jefferson appointed William Hull the new territorial governor, Stanley Griswold, secretary, and Samuel Huntington, Augustus Woodward, and Frederick Bates judges.

Their new capital, Detroit, was still only a small trading town, although it had been in existence for over a hundred years and had been incorporated as a city in 1802.

Before the new governor could reach his capital for the first time, a fire broke out in John Harvey's stable there. The great fire of 1805 spread and people ran from their homes. Before evening almost all of Detroit's buildings lay in a heap of wood ashes, through which ruined and smoking chimneys reached toward the sky.

About two weeks after the fire Governor Hull finally arrived to find his new capital nothing but a ruined heap. Father Gabriel Richard of Detroit, who then was the only clergyman in all of Michigan, surveyed the ruins of the city he loved and said, "We hope for better things; it will arise from its ashes." His words have been used in the present seal of the city of Detroit.

When Judge Woodward arrived, he agreed with Father Richard that this great tragedy might lead to something better. He drew up elaborate plans for a very large and beautiful city, based on the plans of the national capital, Washington, D.C. Although the city never followed the plan to any great extent, some of Detroit is still laid out in the way that Judge Woodward intended. The United States Congress gave Detroit 10,000 acres (more than 4,000 hectares) of land which could be sold for funds to rebuild the city. Gradually, the city was rebuilt.

During the early 1800s Michigan did not experience much growth, although new undertakings were going forward. John Jacob Astor established his American Fur Company headquarters at Mackinac Island in 1808, and this was one of the sources of his great wealth.

By this time, the United States was having constant and increasing trouble with Great Britain. The English never lost an opportunity to stir up the Indians against the Americans.

In 1812 the trouble between Britain and the United States turned into a war. Michigan Territory was not ready for war, nor was the rest of the country. Governor Hull, who had been a fine general in the Revolutionary War, was asked to take the military command at Detroit. He refused at first because he felt that Detroit could not be protected as long as the British controlled Lake Erie, but he finally changed his mind.

Before the war had gone on very long, General Hull surrendered Detroit to the British without a fight. Fort Mackinac had already fallen. Hull's reasons for surrendering were questioned, and the American people were bitter about this defeat. General Hull was court martialed and found guilty of neglect of duty and unofficerlike conduct. He received the death sentence, which later was remitted by President James Madison.

But once again, Michigan was in the hands of the British.

British Colonel Henry Proctor was sent to take charge at Detroit. This was a very difficult time for the people of the city. The Indians of the neighborhood gave Detroiters a particularly bad time, stealing and tormenting as much as they could. They even stole the pipes of Father Richard's organ. But the priest managed to get the word to the Indians that this was the flute of the Great Spirit. The Indians wanted nothing to do with such powerful magic, so one night the pipes were replaced as mysteriously as they had disappeared.

It was not until Commodore Oliver Hazard Perry's great victory over the British navy on Lake Erie in 1813 that it was possible for American forces to retake Detroit. Proctor burned the public buildings of Detroit and left the city. Two days later, in September of 1813, General Duncan McArthur brought Detroit back under American control, to the joy of the inhabitants.

This painting by an unknown artist depicts the Raisin River Massacre, which took place during the War of 1812. In January of 1813, near what is now Monroe, Michigan, a group of British and Indians who occupied what was then Frenchtown overpowered a detachment of American troops. Though the British took some American prisoners with them, they left the wounded with the Indians, who massacred them.

The war ended officially with the Treaty of Ghent. Both sides agreed to give up all territories they had conquered and return to the boundaries as they were before the war.

In order to help restore good feelings on both sides, the leading citizens of Detroit gave a dinner party on March 29, 1815. They called this a "Pacification Dinner," and they invited many people from both sides of the border. This act of good will did much to restore the pleasant relations of the people of Michigan with their Canadian neighbors.

Since the War of 1812, there has been little need for defenses on the border between Canada and the United States.

THE TERRITORY

Lewis Cass was made governor of the Michigan Territory in October of 1813. The war had left the people of Michigan, and especially of Detroit, in great want. The government had to bring in food and supplies as quickly as possible.

A government surveyor had reported that most of the land in Michigan was practically worthless, "interminable swamp, miserably poor." Those Americans who wanted government lands looked elsewhere for many years after this report came out in 1815.

Governor Cass was determined to give his territory a better name. After the territory was enlarged in 1818 to include part of present-day Wisconsin and parts of the Upper Peninsula, the governor decided to explore his territories. In 1820 he and his party started their journey.

At the Sault, he found the Indians angry. One of the chiefs even raised a British flag. Governor Cass hurried over to the flag and tore it down, saying he would not permit a foreign flag on American soil. For a time it appeared the Indians might go on the warpath, but they kept the peace. Cass's bravery was one of the reasons for this.

Governor Cass had with him on the trip a number of experts, including Henry R. Schoolcraft, a geologist. Schoolcraft found many valuable minerals on the journey and the report of the trip caused

Lewis Cass, governor of the Michigan Territory from 1813 to 1831, explored a vast area of the lands he governed in 1820. The members of his expedition traveled great distances over land and water (above) to try to disprove a government survey that had claimed the land was worthless. Cass found the country quite different from what the government had claimed, and his reports attracted settlers to the area.

people to change their minds about Michigan. The governor and his party went on to the Mississippi and traveled up the river for about 350 miles (more than 560 kilometers), hoping to find the source, but the coming winter made them turn back. They had made a difficult journey of over 4,000 miles (over 6,400 kilometers), principally by canoe, without losing a man.

Another important event in Michigan history at this time was the arrival of the first steamboat. This was the *Walk-in-the-Water*. When it first came to Detroit, the Indians stared in amazement at this wonderful ship that sailed along majestically with neither oars nor sails. A joke of the day said that the boat moved because a whole school of sturgeon had been put into harnesses and were pulling the boat through the water, swimming below the surface where they could not be seen.

Within a surprisingly short time, many other steamboats had been built, and passengers and freight were moving between Buffalo and Detroit and other Michigan ports on regular schedules. Then in 1825 the Erie Canal opened, providing an easy water route across New York State. People from New England and every other part of the East could then come to Michigan much more easily than to other western lands, and they could bring more of the necessities of life with them by boat than by any overland route.

This advantage attracted settlers to Michigan country, and large numbers began to arrive in the territory. Michigan was beginning to take advantage of her water wonderland.

In 1828 the territorial capitol building at Detroit was completed. Travelers came from miles around to see this structure, which towered over the other buildings of Detroit to the then-amazing height of 140 feet (over 42 meters). That is about the height of a modern fourteen-story building.

Then in 1831 occurred one of the most unusual events in American history. President Andrew Jackson appointed Stevens T. Mason secretary of the Michigan Territory. The territorial governor at that time, George B. Porter, was often away from Michigan, which made Secretary Mason the acting governor and the actual leader of the territory. This would not seem strange except for the fact that Stevens T. Mason was only nineteen years old when he first became acting governor. He is thought to be the youngest man ever to serve in such a post in the United States.

The people of Michigan were greatly upset. They felt that a boy had no business in such a high office, but the young governor quickly convinced both the president and his fellow citizens that he could manage government affairs with skill—even though he was too young to vote. (The minimum voting age was twenty-one.) He promised always to listen to the counsel of older and more experienced men. In 1834, Governor Porter died, and Mason continued as acting governor. Michigan, as a territory, never had another governor.

In 1832, the Indian chief, Black Hawk, stirred up difficulties between his people and the Americans, and Michigan armed for war. There was no fighting in Michigan during the Black Hawk War, but for a while most of the people were afraid it might come.

After Black Hawk had been defeated and had made peace with the American government, he was taken on a tour of the East to impress him with the Americans' power. On his return to the West, in July of 1833, he passed through Detroit. The whole town turned out to celebrate the Fourth of July by seeing this famous warrior.

The dignified old chief wore a long blue coat and spectacles; his head was covered with a magnificent snow-white top hat, and he carried a handsome cane. He paid a call on Acting Governor Mason. He was much different from what many of the people expected.

Although the Black Hawk rebellion brought no battles to Michigan soil, it did bring another tragedy. A steamer with soldiers on board docked at Detroit, and before it was discovered that there was serious illness on board, numerous Detroit people were infected. An epidemic of the feared disease of cholera was started. Many died, and the doctors were not able to keep up with the needs for medical attention.

During the epidemic, Father Gabriel Richard "might be seen clothed in the robes of his high calling, pale and emaciated, with spectacles on his forehead and prayer book in his hand, going from house to house to visit his parishioners, encouraging the well, and administering spiritual consolation to the sick and dying." The disease had almost run its course when Father Richard became infected himself, and the priest, one of Michigan's greatest citizens, died on September 13, 1832. He had worn himself out with his years of labor for his adopted state and with work for his people, particularly during the awful months of the cholera epidemic.

His funeral was attended by more than two thousand people, more than the whole population of the city of Detroit at that time.

"From early morn until dark the church was filled with the multitude who had come from all quarters to take a last glimpse of him. His remains were followed to the grave amid the solemn tolling of all the bells of the city, and followed by a large concourse of citizens of all classes and denomination who evinced the deepest sorrow. . . ."

During the years between 1807 and 1842 the Indians agreed to many treaties, giving up their lands in Michigan. As more land became available and as the value of the forests and minerals became better known, it seemed that nearly everyone wanted to go to Michigan. In the ten years between 1830 and 1840 so many people caught "Michigan fever" that the population increased from 31,000 to 212,000.

The threat of Indian troubles was in the past, and government land was available at low prices. One of the new arrivals, Mrs. Annie B. Jameson, gives an interesting picture of the Michigan frontier in the 1830s.

"The spires and towers of the city of Detroit were seen against the western sky. The schooners at anchor, or dropping into the river—the little canoes flitting across from side to side—the lofty buildings—the enormous steamers—the noisy port, and busy streets, all

An 1834 lithograph of Detroit.

bathed in the light of a sunset such as I had never seen, not even in Italy—almost turned me giddy with excitement. . . . ''

Mrs. Jameson also describes a party of immigrants from Vermont who were headed west. "They have two wagons covered with canvas, a yoke of oxen, and a pair of horses . . . The father is an old Vermont farmer . . . He has with him fifteen children of different ages . . . all are barefoot except the two eldest girls who are uncommonly handsome with fine dark eyes."

One of the pleasures of the people of Detroit in those days was riding back and forth on the ferry to Canada. As Mrs. Jameson described it, "English emigrants and French Canadians; brisk Americans; dark, sad-looking Indians folded in their blankets; farmers, storekeepers . . . over-dressed, long-waisted damsels, attended by their beaux."

A STATE OR NOT?

By 1835 Michigan qualified to become a state. In that year the people of Michigan adopted a state government and elected officers. Stevens T. Mason, who had then reached only twenty-four years of age, was elected the first governor of the state of Michigan, but the United States Congress refused to recognize the new state. This was the only time in the history of the United States when a state government was actually operating over a period of years while the state was not officially admitted to the Union, and while the territorial government was continuing to operate at the same time.

One of the problems that kept Michigan from statehood was the quarrel with Ohio concerning the southern boundary. Both Michigan and Ohio claimed an area west of Lake Erie which includes the city of Toledo. Some misunderstandings had created doubt as to exactly where the boundary had been intended to be. For a while it looked as if the two states would actually go to war to support their claims.

In the end, Michigan gave up the disputed land and accepted the whole western portion of the Upper Peninsula to make up for it. There were many who thought this was a poor bargain for Michigan,

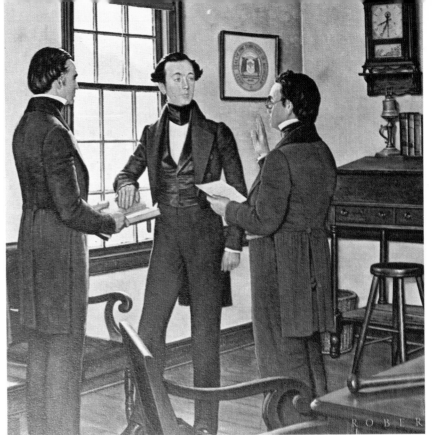

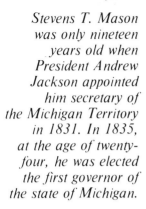

Stevens T. Mason was only nineteen years old when President Andrew Jackson appointed him secretary of the Michigan Territory in 1831. In 1835, at the age of twenty-four, he was elected the first governor of the state of Michigan.

but it was not long before the great mineral wealth of the Upper Peninsula became known. It appeared that Michigan had gained a great deal by "losing" the "border war" with Ohio.

With the settlement of the boundary dispute, Congress was ready to consider Michigan's bid to become a state. But statehood had been delayed for yet another reason. Those who wanted to keep slavery or to enlarge the areas where it was permitted did not want to see Michigan become a state, since it would be a free state, without slavery.

But in 1836, Arkansas was admitted as a slave state, so Congress decided to pair it with a free state. This was done, and Michigan was admitted to full statehood in January of 1837, becoming the twenty-sixth state in the Union.

After so many years as governor in everything but name, Stevens T. Mason took over as governor in actual fact. The two senators and one representative elected by Michigan, who had been trying to get into Congress since 1835, finally were permitted to take their seats.

Yesterday and Today

GOVERNORS, KINGS, AND CAPITALS

The year 1837 was not a very good year for a new state. In fact, it was not a very good year for any state. The country had begun to suffer a depression, and Michigan was especially hard hit. Many banks failed. There was little money; moreover, the state owed five million dollars. Work on canals, railroads, and other public improvements had almost been halted.

To add to the problems, a strange series of events took place in Michigan in 1838. A group of people in Canada wanted to overthrow the British and have an independent Canada. They had many supporters in the United States. These supporters held a mass meeting at Detroit, broke into the Detroit jail and stole arms and ammunition, then seized the schooner *Ann*. They were all ready to attack Canada.

Several times the American friends of the Canadians attempted to go to the aid of their friends in Canada but each time they were kept back. In December of 1838 an American group managed to land above Windsor. They were soon killed or captured.

Governor Mason had a difficult time. He sympathized with the Americans who wanted to help the Canadian rebels, but he was forced to try to keep them in check. United States officials could not permit their people to attack a friendly government.

After two years as governor, the "boy governor" said he would not run for another term, and William Woodbridge was elected the second governor of Michigan. He had been a prominent figure in Michigan history since early territorial days.

Another prominent early Michigan man made an extremely important discovery in 1840. Dr. Douglass Houghton, who was the state geologist, had found important copper deposits in the Upper Peninsula. It had always been thought that large amounts of copper might be found there, but Dr. Houghton's discoveries provided proof of this. These discoveries were to influence Michigan's future more than almost anything else that had happened before.

Only five years later, Dr. Houghton lost his life in a storm on Lake Superior while he was on another voyage of discovery.

A peculiar chapter of Michigan history took place on Beaver Island in Lake Michigan, at about this time. A group of members of the Church of Jesus Christ of Latter Day Saints had settled on the island in 1846. Their leader on Beaver Island was James Jesse Strang, who had himself proclaimed King of the Island. He ruled his followers with an iron hand, maintaining an absolute monarchy in his island domain. This was the first and only time in United States history that anyone has ruled in such a fashion.

Because these Mormons, as members of this church are called, had different religious practices from most of the people, they had a difficult time wherever they settled. This was especially true when they had a "king." Feelings finally grew so high on Beaver Island that there was a "battle" in 1854 between the Mormon settlers and Irish settlers of the area.

In 1856, Strang was assassinated. Mobs from the mainland forced the Mormons off the island and took their property. Today there are only a few memories of King James the First.

Just a year after the Mormons settled on Beaver Island, another group of settlers came to Michigan. These were the Dutch, refugees from religious persecution in Holland, who founded Holland, Michigan, in 1847. After many difficulties and disasters, the hard-working Dutch settlers finally became successful in maintaining their community, and they remain so today.

Until this time Detroit had remained not only the principal city but the capital of Michigan. Now, however, the state legislature had decided to move the capital to another location. But so many of the lawmakers had their own favorite cities it was impossible to select one.

Finally, they decided they would have to select a location that was not connected with any of the legislators, and in 1847 Lansing was chosen to be the new capital. People could hardly believe that their new capital was to be in the heart of a woodland wilderness where there was only one log house and a sawmill. The new capital had no roads, and could only be reached by an Indian trail.

On January 3, 1848, Michigan's capital was moved from Detroit to Lansing.

Nevertheless, the capital was moved to Lansing in January of 1848. Lansing became known as "the capital in the forest." The first capitol building was built of the wonderful walnut trees from the nearby woodlands.

THE ISSUE OF SLAVERY

By this time the people of Michigan were concerned with a problem that was becoming more serious every day as opinion among the people of the United States was more and more widely split. This was the problem of slavery.

35

*Michigan's present great capitol is a far
cry from the first one "in the forest."*

The abolitionists, who wanted to abolish slavery, were strong in Michigan. Many Michigan people helped slaves to escape to Canada over a system of hideouts known as the "Underground Railroad."

The abolitionists were also dissatisfied with the old political parties. In 1854 a group of anti-slavery people called a meeting at Jackson, Michigan, to establish a new political party in which they felt they could have confidence.

So many people came to Jackson that there was no building large enough to hold the crowd. They met outdoors in what has been called the "Convention Under the Oaks," and chose the name Republican for their party. Several states claim to have been the birthplace of the national Republican party. Among these, Michigan has one of the strongest claims because of the convention at Jackson on July 6, 1854.

Michigan has an even firmer position in the beginning of the Republican party because of the election of 1854. Michigan's Republicans won the election, and Michigan was the first state to have a Republican governor, Kingsley Bingham. The Republicans also won three of Michigan's four seats in the United States House of Representatives, as well as both houses of the state legislature.

Neither Republicans nor Democrats could keep the arguments over slavery from becoming stronger as the years went by. At last the horrors of civil war came to a country that was not prepared for it.

During the first year of fighting, twenty-one Michigan regiments were formed. Michigan men fought in most of the early battles of the war in the East, when most people thought the war would be over in a few months at the most.

As the war went on, Michigan soldiers gained a reputation for their courage. Among the most heroic of these were the men of the Michigan Cavalry Brigade led by General George Armstrong Custer. This brigade played a key part in the Confederate defeat at Gettysburg.

Soldiers of the Michigan Engineers and Mechanics took an important part in another prominent operation of the war. The Union troops in Chattanooga were surrounded by Confederates and would have starved for lack of supplies. Just in time, the Union armies were able to build a road and a pontoon bridge to reach their forces in Chattanooga. The Michigan Engineers placed the bridge in position over the Tennessee River, and it was given the name "Michigan Bridge."

In helping to take Missionary Ridge near Chattanooga, the 11th Michigan Infantry performed one of the most spectacular charges of the whole war.

A brave Michigan boy, Charles Howard Gardner, began serving in the Civil War at the age of twelve to keep from being separated from his teacher.

A few women also fought in the Civil War. The most famous female soldier from Michigan was Sarah Emma Edmonds. She enlisted as Franklin Thompson and concealed her identity for two years. She fought with the Second Michigan Infantry in four major campaigns, and as a spy narrowly escaped with her life several times. Her most successful "disguise" as a spy was that of a woman.

At the end of the war, the Fourth Michigan Cavalry became one of the most famous outfits in either army by carrying out the outstanding capture of the war. They discovered the camp where Jefferson Davis, the president of the Confederacy, was hiding, took him prisoner, and brought their famous captive to federal authorities.

A total of 92,000 Michigan soldiers had served in the Civil War—a very large percentage of a state with such a small population as Michigan then had. Fourteen thousand Michigan soldiers lost their lives in battle and 10,000 more died of disease. Many Michigan soldiers received the nation's highest honor, the Congressional Medal of Honor, but two men from Michigan received it twice. These were Thomas W. Custer, brother of General George Custer, and Frank D. Baldwin.

AFTER THE WAR

On the same day as the great Chicago fire, October 8, 1871, a great fire swept across Michigan, killing more people than did the Chicago

The 24th Michigan Infantry Regiment (above) fought bravely and incurred great losses at Gettysburg on July 1, 1863.

fire. The strong winds united several Michigan brush fires, and swept rapidly through the Michigan timber. Holland, Michigan, was destroyed just as it was preparing to celebrate its twenty-fifth anniversary. Manistee was partially destroyed, and the fire swept clear across the state. Eighteen thousand Michigan people were left without homes.

While fire was devouring so much of the Michigan forests, at the very same time fire was destroying the wooden buildings of Chicago, which had been built almost entirely of white pine from the Michigan woodlands.

Ten years later, another Michigan forest fire swept across a very large area and killed 125 people.

Michigan was one of the first states in which labor unions formed and grew. In 1885, Michigan working people won one of their greatest victories when a law was passed declaring ten hours as a legal day's work. Before that, people were sometimes required to work as much as sixteen or eighteen hours a day. The labor-union movement has remained strong in Michigan to this day.

In 1897, Hazen S. Pingree, one of the state's most popular politicians, became governor of Michigan. When he was elected governor, he was also mayor of Detroit. He kept both of those positions until the state Supreme Court ruled that he could retain only one post, so he resigned as mayor.

During this same period, several Michigan men became interested in a new activity that was to change the whole course of life for Michigan and its people, and for the whole world. This was the automobile industry, which will be covered in detail in a later section.

Michigan's contribution to transportation revolutionized not only the state but the world. This is a portion of the Greenfield Village automobile collection.

INTO THE TWENTIETH CENTURY

The war known as World War I began in Europe in 1914. Although the United States did not actually enter the war against Germany until 1917, Detroit became the center of much German spy activity. When the United States did come into the war, the soldiers of the 32nd Division became the first American troops on German soil, although this did not take place until the war was nearing its end. The 32nd contained one of the largest groups of Michigan soldiers in any division.

After the war, changes came quickly. William B. Stout produced the first all-metal airplane in the United States. Working with Henry Ford, he later developed this plane into the famous Ford trimotor, which was a great influence in developing commercial air travel. Some of the old Ford trimotors are still flying today, after more than fifty years. Michigan has played a key part in developing nearly all modern forms of transportation.

DEPRESSION AND MID-CENTURY

The Great Depression of 1929 had a worse effect on Michigan than on many other states, because so many people in Michigan depended on industry. During the depression, few people had money to buy automobiles and Michigan's other major products, so unemployment in the state was particularly serious.

The country was not yet over the effects of the depression when another war began—a war which was to be the worst in history.

An enormous total of 673,000 Michigan men and women served in the United States armed forces during World War II. The Red Arrow Division, which included a large percentage of Michigan men, was one of the first American groups to meet the Japanese in the South Pacific. The Red Arrow's combat record of 654 days has never been equaled.

During the war, the Sault Ste. Marie area was the most heavily guarded spot in the United States. If the enemy had been able to destroy the locks there, they might have crippled a large part of the country's war manufacturing.

In World War II, the factories of Michigan produced the unbelievable total of one-eighth of all the war materiel produced in the whole United States. This record far surpassed that of any other state. For the war, Michigan produced a total of twenty-seven billion dollars worth of munitions.

The Willow Run plant of the Ford Motor Company could build a B-24 bomber every hour. The Defoe Company became the region's largest producer of fighting boats. They developed a new method of production permitting them to turn out a complete boat every week.

Even Michigan children did their part. Michigan's young people contributed the money that purchased a glider. This glider later became the first to land in Normandy on the great invasion of Europe by American and other Allied forces on D-Day—June 6, 1944.

Only a few years later, in 1950, the Michigan National Guard sent the first American unit into action in the Korean War.

"BIG MAC"

Michigan has been a divided state. The upper and lower parts of Michigan are split by the Straits of Mackinac, connecting lakes Huron and Michigan. This has been good for water transportation between the two lakes, but has made it difficult to get from one part of the state to the other.

Of course, there were ferries to carry people and cars across the straits. But on busy days, it was sometimes necessary to wait in line for hours to board a ferry for the trip between the two peninsulas of Michigan.

For years people had dreamed of linking these peninsulas with a bridge, but the distance was so great (about five miles or eight kilometers), the straits were so deep, and currents of water and wind were so strong that most plans for bridges seemed too difficult and expensive.

"Big Mac," the bridge linking the upper and lower parts of Michigan, was completed in 1957.

Then at last suitable plans were made, the builders got the go-ahead, and a really wonderful structure was completed in 1957. Someone said, "The North and the South of the state have long been engaged. Now they had a wedding ring." At the dedication of the bridge, Governor G. Mennen Williams called it "another Northwest Passage."

"Big Mac," as the bridge is known to almost everyone, had cost one hundred million dollars. Its distance of 8,614 feet (2,625.55 meters) between cable anchorages is the fourth-longest of any suspension bridge in the world. It has become one of the great tourist attractions of Michigan.

In 1967 riots occurred that destroyed many buildings in the inner city of Detroit. Since that time, much rebuilding has taken place. In the 1970s the Renaissance Center, a hotel and office complex on Detroit's riverfront, was completed.

Because the state is so dependent on the auto industry, depressions have an especially severe effect in Michigan. One of the most severe was the decline of auto sales in late 1975, followed by a record recovery in 1976.

Natural Treasures

GROWING THINGS

Michigan has received many gifts from nature. Some could easily be seen even by the first explorers—forests, fresh water, and valuable fur animals.

The great forests of Michigan covered most of the state. Even today, almost twenty million acres (more than eight million hectares) of land in Michigan are covered with trees. This is still more than half of the state's land area. Much of the state is being reforested. Twenty million seedling pines are planted each year in Michigan.

There are eighty-five varieties of trees in Michigan—more than in any other state and more than in all of Europe. Michigan has many of the largest trees of various kinds to be found anywhere in the country. Near Ironwood, a white pine almost 18 feet (almost 5.5 meters) in circumference is found. A black walnut near New Haven is 12 feet, 8 inches (3.86 meters) in circumference, and there are many other trees of record size in Michigan.

MINERALS AND MINING

Copper was another of Michigan's natural treasures that the early Europeans in Michigan saw in a few areas. Some wonderful pieces of copper were found right on the surface of the ground. The most famous of these was the huge Ontonagon Boulder, larger than any ever seen before.

Over the years, many Indians and several Europeans had seen this valuable rock. In 1843 Julius Eldred went up the Ontonagon River, where the copper boulder was located. He had to use a block and

Opposite: The shifting sands of Sleeping Bear Dunes are slowly uncovering a vast stand of timber along the Lake Michigan shore.

45

tackle and build a small railroad to the river to get the boulder out, but he was sure people would pay money to see this wondrous rock, so he eventually moved the metal lump to Detroit and put it on exhibition.

There the United States government seized it, although Eldred was supposed to have had government permission to take it. The United States officials took it to Washington, D.C., where it can still be seen in the Natural History Building of the National Museum.

The publicity about the Ontonagon Boulder interested many people in the possibilities of copper mining in Michigan.

Today, copper is still important in Michigan. The deposits of copper are among the most important anywhere. The body of copper ore in the White Pine Region is thought to be the largest copper reserve in America.

This diorama from the University of Michigan Exhibit Museum shows Old Copper Culture people mining copper.

Cross-country skiing in copper country, at Fort Wilkins, near Copper Harbor.

Michigan has more than 220,000,000 tons (199,581,000 metric tons) of coal and a billion tons (907,185,000 metric tons) of peat in its reserves.

There are very large reserves of thorium available, if that metal ever becomes important in the production of atomic energy.

Great quantities of iron ore have been found in Michigan. The highest-quality iron ore has already been mined. The iron that remains is generally of lower quality. Much of it cannot be mined profitably at the present time, but new methods of preparing the ore and future needs for more ore may some day make its greater use possible.

THE PROTECTED LIFE

The state has been famous for many of its birds. The very rare kirtland, or Jack Pine warbler, is still to be found around Mio. But one of the most famous of all birds will never be seen again.

The passenger pigeon was a beautiful bird, about 15 inches (38 centimeters) long. It came to Michigan early in March from its winter quarters. At one time there were probably more passenger pigeons than any other bird. During the great migrating flights of these birds, they flew so close together they darkened the sky. It sometimes took hours for a single flock to pass over a given spot.

Commercial hunters and so-called sportsmen killed passenger pigeons by the millions. A live pigeon was tied to a stool as a decoy. When the stool was moved the bird would flap its wings and attract hundreds of other birds, which would then be killed. This was the beginning of the term "stool pigeon."

One of the largest known gatherings of passenger pigeons took place near Petoskey in March of 1878. The beech trees where they roosted were weighted down so heavily with birds that branches throughout the woods could be heard snapping off under the weight. Hunters killed or captured more than a million pigeons at that time and place.

The killing continued until forty years later there was not a single passenger pigeon in existence. Every one of the millions had been killed. No one had thought to save any of these birds, and now the passenger pigeon is completely extinct.

Because they are now carefully protected, other game birds, such as the quail, ruffed grouse, and prairie chicken, are still to be found. Huron County claims to have the finest pheasants in the United States, although pheasants are not native to this country.

Michigan has also long been noted for the many varieties of fish in its many rivers and lakes, as well as in the Great Lakes.

One of Michigan's most famous and beautiful fish, the grayling trout, was caught in such quantities that it, too, became extinct in the 1930s. Now, however, Michigan has one of the most successful and complete programs for the protection of its valuable plants and wildlife. In 1881 Michigan was the first state to pay a state game warden.

Due to its wonderful forests, Michigan has had a fine variety of animals. One of the state's nicknames is the "Wolverine State," yet in spite of this nickname, it is doubtful wolverines lived there in very large numbers, possibly never.

The otter, opossum, black bear, raccoon, weasel, mink, skunk, badger, coyote, timber wolf, red fox, bobcat, woodchuck, beaver, muskrat, porcupine, deer, and rabbit are found in Michigan now, or have been found there at one time. Moose and elk were once found in the state in considerable numbers. The marten, woodland caribou, cougar, and bison no longer are found in the state, according to most experts.

One interesting event concerning animals in Michigan took place in 1912. For the first time in recorded history, Lake Superior froze over so solidly that moose, and possibly wolves, crossed the ice from the mainland to Isle Royale in the middle of the lake. They had not been known there before.

This flock of wild swans winter on a farm pond in Bellaire as part of Michigan's wildlife habitat management program. The state has one of the most successful and complete programs for the protection of its valuable plants and wildlife.

Michigan's fields and forests contributed to the life of the Indian peoples, as shown in this diorama of a Potawatomi fall harvest, and the wealth of the forests and soils still pour out for the people today.

The People Use Their Treasures

FURS AND FISH

Before Europeans came to Michigan, Indians lived throughout the state. They fashioned incredibly efficient bark canoes, which would carry thirty times their own weight even in shallow water. The Indians also made snowshoes, clothing that was ideally suited to Michigan's many climate variations, and simple tools and implements. They grew some crops and evaporated the salt from Michigan's many salt springs.

When the Europeans first arrived, they were most interested in the beavers. Skins of these animals were much in demand in Europe. For most of the earlier years of Michigan's history, the fur trade was about the only commerce in the area. Beaver skins were so valuable that they sometimes were used for money.

So many beavers were caught and killed that of course they became scarce. Fortunately, precautions were taken to save the beaver before this interesting and intelligent animal followed the passenger pigeon and the grayling trout into extinction. In 1920 the hunting or trapping of beavers was forbidden. By 1934 the beaver population had increased enough that some beavers were allowed to be killed, and this policy has been continued. In Michigan today there are several thousand licensed trappers.

The "water wonderland" of Michigan also provides another source of wealth. Over twelve million tons (nearly eleven million metric tons) of fish are pulled from the state's sparkling waters each year for commercial purposes. This is in addition to all the sport fishing in the state.

FORTUNES IN TREES

A growing United States needed lumber, and so thousands of people went to the Michigan forests hoping to make their fortunes there. In the years between 1840 and 1900, enough lumber to make ten

Timbering in Bellaire.

million six-room houses came out of Michigan's standing pine timber. A huge amount of lumber was cut from Michigan's cedar, hemlock, and other hardwood trees during the same period.

The lumber cut in Michigan during that sixty-year period was enough to cover the whole state with a floor one inch (2.5 centimeters) thick, adding the area of Rhode Island for good measure.

Michigan's trees came to be called "green gold." Even at a low estimate, the green gold of Michigan was worth far more than the yellow gold of California, which caused the famous gold rush of 1849. At least a billion dollars more came from Michigan's lumber than from California's gold. In the period from 1840 to 1900, the value of Michigan's lumber has been placed at $2.25 billion.

The Michigan lumber camps and the strong-willed workers in them became famous, and the tales of the camps have added their own new section to our national folklore. Stories of the giant imaginary lumberman, Paul Bunyan, and his blue ox, Babe, were set in the forests and lumber camps of the state of Michigan.

52

During the logging season, the rivers of the state were clogged with giant trunks being floated down to the sawmills.

By 1873 there were more than 1,600 sawmills in the state of Michigan alone. Lumber towns grew large and prosperous. Saginaw was once called the "Timber Capital of the World."

Several Michigan residents grew so wealthy and powerful in the lumber business they came to be known as "lumber barons." They competed desperately to get control of the best timber lands.

By 1900 most of the best white pine forests had been destroyed completely. Desolate acres (hectares) were covered with stumps or burned-over blackness, or barren sand wastes. Many lumbermen moved on to other states. Once-prosperous towns were deserted and became ghost towns. When farmers tried to use the land, they found that much of it was not suitable for farming.

Since that unfortunate time, however, Michigan has accomplished much in restoring its forest lands and preserving and building up its remaining timber tracts. Lumbering is still an important industry, worth sixty million dollars a year to the state. There are still more than 400 saw, paper, pulp, and veneer mills in Michigan, most of

Log storage basin on the St. Marys River.

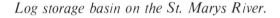

them in the Upper Peninsula. Almost twenty million acres (over eight million hectares) in Michigan remain forested. There are twenty-three state forests and five national forests in Michigan today.

Most of the world's supply of birdseye maple comes from Michigan. A tremendous amount of this beautiful wood was used in decorating the steamship *Queen Mary* when it was built in 1936.

FORTUNES IN THE GROUND

The first person to discover the mineral wealth of Michigan was the state geologist, Dr. Douglass Houghton. In 1843 there was a great mining rush because of Dr. Houghton's discoveries of copper deposits. The town of Houghton, named for him, became the first American mining "boom town." In the period between 1847 and 1887, Michigan was the leading producer of copper in the United States. Important copper deposits are still being worked in the state.

One of the pioneers in Michigan's iron mining was named John Wood. He was so important in the iron-mining industry that he received the nickname "Iron." This, added to his own last name, gave the city of Ironwood its name.

Today, the Mather Iron Mine is one of the world's largest underground mines. The city of Escanaba is the only ore shipping point on Lake Michigan.

Mining in Michigan, which except for salt is almost all concentrated in the Upper Peninsula, still earns hundreds of millions of dollars a year.

Michigan has also refined and used much of its own iron ore. In 1864, for the first time in the United States, steel ingots were made by the Bessemer process at the Eureka Iron Works owned by Eber Brock Ward in Wyandotte. In 1885 the first steel rails made in the United States were produced at Ironwood.

One of the earliest of all mineral industries is still an important one in Michigan. The state is the country's largest producer of salt. Twenty-nine percent of the nation's salt deposits are found in the state. The sixty miles (nearly ninety-seven kilometers) of tunnels in the International Salt Company's mines would hold the entire population of Detroit.

Manistee is one of the world's largest producers of salt, and the Dow Chemical Company at Midland, Michigan, is one of the world's largest chemical companies. It depends on the salts and related basic chemicals found in its region.

A little-known fact is that Michigan produces both oil and natural gas. Gas and oil had been discovered near Howell by 1834, but it was not until the 1920s that they became important in Michigan. Today there are almost four thousand wells producing oil or gas in the state. Carefully regulated, oil will continue to be one source of wealth for the people of Michigan for many years to come.

THE SOIL BRINGS FORTH

Although it is not among the leading five states in agriculture, Michigan ranks high in many crops, especially a number of unusual crops that are not grown in many other states.

Michigan is the largest producer of mint in the United States. The peppermint industry is centered around St. Johns. Mint is cut like hay, left for thirty-six hours to cure in the sun, and then hauled to the still. There the fragrant mint oil is taken from the leaves. In addition to peppermint, spearmint is an important mint crop in Michigan.

As much as 96 percent of the navy beans grown in the United States are produced in Michigan's rustling bean fields. In tribute to the beans of Michigan, in 1904 the Speaker of the United States House of Respresentatives, Joseph Cannon, successfully put through a bill to serve navy bean soup every day in the Capitol restaurant.

Half of all the sour cherries in the United States are produced in Michigan. Traverse City is probably the largest cherry-marketing center in the United States. Most of this industry started from one orchard planted in the 1880s. A cherry blossom festival is held every spring at Traverse City.

The state is also first in the growing of cucumbers and blueberries. It ranks second in strawberries, plums, and asparagus for processing, and third in its crops of apples, pears, grapes, and celery. Kalamazoo is sometimes called the "celery city," for the city was the birthplace of America's celery production. Benton Harbor has the world's largest non-citrus fruit and vegetable market.

The state produces more seedling evergreens than any other. Wheat, hay, oats, turkeys, hogs, and beef cattle are other important products of Michigan farms. In spite of all the water surrounding the state, there are 2,000 irrigated farms in Michigan. The "Thumb" (the Saginaw-Bay City area) is an especially rich farming region.

Altogether, the state ranks twenty-first among all the states in agriculture.

MANUFACTURING MAGIC

Michigan is always associated with at least three outstanding products—automobiles, breakfast food, and furniture.

The wonderful hardwoods of Michigan are particularly suitable for furniture making. In 1836 William Haldane arrived in Grand Rapids. He was an excellent cabinet maker, and the first in the city's long line of furniture manufacturers. Many Haldane chairs of black walnut are still in use today.

In 1876 the furniture manufacturers from Grand Rapids showed their furniture at the Centennial Exposition in Philadelphia. The response to their exhibit was so great that they could not keep up with the orders. Since that time Grand Rapids has represented furniture to many people.

The town of Battle Creek is most often associated with cereals. Two unusual men, Will Keith Kellogg and C.W. Post, were pioneers in the manufacture of processed breakfast foods. Both worked in Michigan. Today the Post plant and the Kellogg plant in Battle Creek are the largest of their type anywhere. Through the funds of the Kellogg Foundation, established by W.K. Kellogg, many worthwhile causes in the arts and in education have received much-needed help.

Michigan leads all other states in the manufacture of automobile parts, as well as trailers, boats, engines, refrigerators, and office equipment. The stove and furnace industry is also one of the important manufacturing interests of the state.

The world's largest cement plant is in Alpena. Grindstone City, which still produces grindstones, once held a near monopoly on the making of grindstones. The world's largest limestone quarry is in Presque Isle, and the Bear Archery Company is the world's largest manufacturer of archery products.

Because so much of the equipment used by magicians is manufactured at Colon, that city has come to be known as the magic capital of the world.

Other important Michigan products include aspirin, baby food, and carpet sweepers. More aspirin is produced in Michigan than in any other state. The first and largest canner of baby foods is the Gerber Company, located in Fremont. In Grand Rapids is the Bissel factory, the largest manufacturer of carpet sweepers.

More recently, Michigan's factories have entered the space age. Redstone boosters and Jupiter missiles have been made at Chrysler factories located just outside Detroit. Guided-missile destroyers are made at the Defoe Ship Company in Bay City, and other computer and avionic products are made in various factories around the state.

Altogether, more than 2,200 different manufactured products could bear a label that says, "Made in Michigan," and Michigan is the sixth most important state in manufacturing.

Another important industry in Michigan is based on the myriad interesting things to see and do in the state. The tourist business in Michigan brings in about a billion dollars, and Michigan greets more than nine million visitors from other states each year.

WHEN HORSEPOWER REPLACED HORSES

Another Michigan city whose name is associated with a particular industry is, of course, Detroit. The people of that city "remade America with the automobile," according to Raymond C. Miller,

Norman Rockwell's painting of Henry Ford working on his first car, the 1896 Quadricycle, in his Bagley Avenue workshop, as his wife watches.

"and then remade the world with the techniques they have learned in the automobile plants."

The first self-propelled vehicle in Michigan was probably the steam-driven car of John and Thomas Clegg, built in their machine shop at Memphis in the winter of 1884-1885. Ransom E. Olds built a three-wheel steam car in 1887 and drove it around Lansing.

A gasoline-engine car, seen on the streets of Detroit in 1896, was built by Charles G. King.

Norman Rockwell's painting of Henry Ford driving his 1903 Ford car on a Detroit street.

The Detroit *News-Tribune* of February 4, 1900, featured an article called, "Thrilling Trip on the First Detroit-Made Automobile." This was the car built by a then almost unknown man named Henry Ford. He was chief engineer at the new Detroit Automobile Company.

The writer of the article said, "Looking over the latest Detroit automobile, a good impression was created. Smooth covered, box-topped, with black enameled sides, red wheels and running gear, nothing but the absence of the proverbial horse revealed the motive power was to come from within . . . Beyond all doubt, the automobileer—is that the new word?—will be the most important manager this coming century. He sits on a little seat, in front; and by pulling a lever and by pressing a small button in the floor, with his foot, he controls the thing with all the confidence imaginable.

"The machine runs, stops and backs at his will. He turns sharp curves with the grace and ease of a wild bird under full sail."

At this time, Michigan was mostly a rural state, with very few people interested in anything like a "horseless carriage."

Detroit was one of the leaders of the horse-carriage business, so there was a background industry for the new automobile trade. But it is probably the leadership of the Detroit automobile pioneers that put the city on the road to leadership in the industry.

The fact that the state quickly became a leader in mass production was also very important. Ransom E. Olds was a pioneer in auto mass production. In 1904 he turned out five thousand of his "Oldsmobiles" at his new plant in Lansing. Later he formed the REO Company, using the initials of his name for the name of his new car, the Reo.

Henry Ford was associated with three companies before he became successful with his Ford Motor Company.

The year 1908 was one of the most important in the history of the automobile. In that year Ford brought out his Model T, and in that same year the General Motors Corporation, now the world's largest manufacturing organization, was formed in Detroit.

Over the years Detroit has been home to more than 170 auto manufacturers. Most of the cars produced bore the names of the founders of the companies. Most of these names are gone from the streets today, although some—Ford, Chevrolet, Oldsmobile, Buick, and Dodge—are still leaders.

Ford and his Model T remained leaders in the auto industry for many years. Then the Model T became outdated and began to lose sales to its competition, particularly Chevrolet. So Ford brought out his Model A, and finally the V-8. The Ford River Rouge plant in Dearborn is the largest industrial unit in the world not owned by a government.

60

*Proud owners of a 1908 Model T touring car
visit friends on a farm. Norman Rockwell.*

It was not until 1925 that the last of the "Big Three" automobile companies came into being. In that year Walter P. Chrysler, who had been with General Motors, set up his own company. Not very much later he also took control of the very successful Dodge company, after the death of the Dodge Brothers who had founded the company.

As the home of the "Big Three," Michigan produces more motor vehicles than any other place in the world. Eighty-five percent of all cars, trucks, and other automotive vehicles made in the United

*Above: Modern Ford assembly plant continues the
state's pioneering in automobile production.
Below: Aerial view of the Ford Motor Company's River Rouge plant.*

States are produced by Michigan-based companies. In 1935 the United Automobile Workers, one of the nation's largest labor unions, was organized with headquarters in Detroit.

TRANSPORTATION AND COMMUNICATION

On all of the upper Great Lakes there was only one closed door. Lake Superior is 22 feet (6.7 meters) higher than the other Great Lakes. The rapids of the St. Marys River, where the Pageant of the Soo took place more than three hundred years ago, carry the waters of the river down from the level of Lake Superior. No ship can go up those rocky rapids, and only canoes and kayaks can shoot down them. Early European visitors often watched in awe as the Indians shot the rapids of the Soo in their frail canoes.

There was only one way to get from the other lakes to the level of Lake Superior—boats and all their cargo had to be portaged on land to the up side of the rapids.

Some large ships were hauled over the portage on rollers. It took the schooner *Algonquin* a good part of the winter of 1839-1840 to move slowly upstream on the land, around the rapids. The steamboats *Independence* and *Julia Palmer* made the difficult haul in 1846. A few fair-sized boats had been built on Lake Superior and for a time they were all that was needed.

In 1850 a horse-drawn tramway began to carry cargo around the Soo rapids.

Then with the rapid growth of the mining around Lake Superior, it was apparent that a canal and locks were needed. There had once been a canal with a lock, built on the Canadian side in 1797. This was big enough for canoes and small boats, towed by oxen, but the canal and lock had been destroyed by the Americans during the War of 1812.

To most people, building a tremendous engineering work in the middle of a wilderness seemed ridiculous. But some members of the Michigan legislature and some members of the United States Congress were able to see how a canal would benefit everyone in the

*The Soo Locks still provide one of the world's
most important transportation links.*

future, and plans for a canal and locks were approved. Charles T.
Harvey, an agent for the Fairbanks Scale Company, convinced his
company to take the contract to build the canal and locks. In spite of
great difficulties, Harvey finished the canal and locks on schedule, in
1855.

The canal was just over a mile (1.6 kilometers) long and 100 feet
(30.48 meters) wide. Two locks, 350 feet (106.68 meters) long and
70 feet (21.34 meters) wide, lay side by side. They were capable of
raising and lowering ships 18 feet (5.49 meters). The cost of the
canal was just under a million dollars.

At last, trade could be carried entirely by water from the farthest reaches of the Great Lakes to the Atlantic Ocean, using the Erie Canal in New York State. The steamer *Illinois* was the first to pass through the locks, traveling westward. Later the same day the steamer *Baltimore* made the passage down to Lake Huron.

Over the years, more locks were built and older locks replaced. Today there are four American locks and one Canadian. Some of the freighters handled there are more than 700 feet (more than 200 meters) long.

The Soo Canal today is by far the busiest canal in the world. This waterway is probably most responsible for the fact that in the late 1800s the United States became the greatest manufacturing nation in the world and has remained so ever since.

Around the Great Lakes are all the basic raw materials needed by great industries: iron ore, coal, limestone, copper, and many others. Using the Soo Canal, all of these materials can be brought together in great quantities at low cost for processing. Nowhere else in the world is this possible in just the same way or on so great a scale. Even Charles Harvey might have been somewhat surprised at the results of his dream of pushing through a canal in the wilderness.

Today, the canal and locks are also among the great tourist attractions of the world.

Other waterways have kept pace. The Detroit River has long been the busiest waterway in the world. It carries more tonnage than any other shipping lane.

The opening of the St. Lawrence Seaway in 1959 brought Detroit and all the Great Lakes ports within the reach of most of the world's oceangoing freighters. Forty lake ports in Michigan are served by freighters and passenger ships. Nineteen of the state's ports handle more than a million tons (nearly a million metric tons) of freight each year. No other state has as many million-ton ports.

Michigan has been a leader in other forms of transportation and communication. Its first railroad, the Erie and Kalamazoo, began operating between Adrian, Michigan, and Toledo, Ohio, in 1836.

With its interest in automobiles, it is natural that Michigan has been a pioneer in building roads. In the early days it had the most plank roads of any state, and claims that the world's first concrete road was laid in Detroit in 1909. Today the state's highways are among the nation's finest. None of Michigan's highways, except the Mackinac Bridge and the crossings to Canada, charge tolls.

The nation's first regularly scheduled passenger air service began in Michigan in 1926. It flew between Detroit and Grand Rapids.

The first book printed in the whole Northwest Territory was published in Detroit in 1809, by the press established by Father Gabriel Richard. This press printed fifty-two books during its existence. The first successful newspaper in Michigan, the *Detroit Gazette,* was published from 1817 until 1830.

Detroit was also an important force in early radio broadcasting. Station WWJ produced the first news broadcast in history on August 31, 1920. This station also was responsible for the first broadcast of singing, the first church services on the air, and the first dance band to be heard on radio—Fred Waring and his Pennsylvanians.

Visitors to Greenfield Village experience an early form of transportation behind this century-old steam engine.

Human Treasures

There are many people associated with Michigan whose names are known throughout the world. Others who may have made even more important contributions to the state are generally not well known outside of Michigan.

One of the latter is Father Gabriel Richard. From the time he first was assigned to Detroit in 1798 until his death, Father Richard took a leading part in almost every worthwhile activity of his adopted town, in addition to ministering to the needs of his parish.

His Bishop wrote of Father Richard: "He has a talent of doing, almost at the same time, ten things entirely different. In charge of the newspaper, aware of all political news, always ready to discuss religion when the opportunity offers and very well equipped in theology, he makes hay, gathers the fruits of his garden, picks up a peach on the ground before him, teaches one young fellow mathematics, shows another how to read, says a prayer, establishes a printing press, confesses everybody, brings over carding machines, a spinning jenny, and looms to teach his parishioners how to work them, keeps his records up-to-date, demonstrates an electrical machine, visits the sick at a great distance, writes and receives letters from everywhere, preaches every Sunday and feast day, at length and wisely, adds to his library, spends the nights without sleep, is on the go all day long, loves to talk, sees company, catechises his young parishioners, looks after a school for girls, carries himself well, as well physically at the age of fifty as most men are at thirty. . . ."

Father Richard printed the first book in Michigan and published the first newspaper. Until a Protestant minister came, he held services for the Protestants of the area.

During the War of 1812, the British arrested Father Richard. But they soon freed him at the request of their ally, the great Indian chief Tecumseh.

In one of his many efforts to aid education, Father Richard helped to prepare the way for the founding of the University of Michigan in 1817. In 1823 Father Richard was elected the representative of Michigan Territory in the Congress at Washington.

Father Richard, as someone has said, "was, in his humble way, an empire builder." Others have called Father Gabriel Richard "the patron saint of Detroit."

Another priest, who spent much of his life in the wilds of the Upper Peninsula, was Father Frederic Baraja. During his many years of missionary work with the Indians he translated a hymn book into the Chippewa language and compiled a Chippewa dictionary. He was called "the parish priest of Lake Superior." Finally he was made bishop of the region, with headquarters at Sault Ste. Marie, and later at Marquette.

PUBLIC FIGURES

The second governor of Michigan Territory, Lewis Cass, was also a young man, although not as young as Governor Stevens T. Mason, who later became the first governor of Michigan as a state. Governor Cass was only thirty-one when he became the chief executive of Michigan Territory. He served for eighteen years in that post. Later he served the nation as United States Senator, as United States Secretary of War, and as Minister to France. He became a candidate for President in 1848, but was defeated by Zachary Taylor.

Another Michigan man who was twice a candidate for the office of president of the United States was Thomas E. Dewey, born in Owosso. He gained his early fame in New York, where he became a prominent governor of that state. As the Republican candidate, he was defeated in the race for president by Franklin D. Roosevelt and later by Harry Truman.

Michigan finally had a president of its own in 1974. At that time Gerald R. Ford, for many years a congressman from Grand Rapids, became president when Richard M. Nixon resigned. President Ford had been appointed vice-president a few months before when the former vice-president, Spiro T. Agnew, resigned. Ford ran unsuccessfully for a full term in office in 1976.

Ralph J. Bunche, born in Detroit, received the Nobel Peace Prize in 1950 for his work in the United Nations.

One of Michigan's most prominent military men was General George Armstrong Custer, who became a national hero during the Civil War. He was made a general at the amazingly early age of twenty-three. He and his men are generally credited with helping to turn the tide of battle at Gettysburg.

Later, as the commander of United States Indian fighters, General Custer became the central figure in what we call "Custer's last stand." He and 225 of his men were killed on the desolate banks of the Little Big Horn River in Montana. Not a man was spared, and the dead included Custer's two brothers, his nephew, and a brother-in-law. Today a national cemetery covers with green the area where the massacre took place in 1876.

This was a dramatic end to a notable military record. Sadly, however, military authorities today hold Custer responsible for the tragedy and say that it probably could have been avoided with the proper action on the general's part.

MERCHANT PRINCES

Several merchandising giants have been associated with Michigan. Sebastian S. Kresge of Detroit founded the great Kresge variety store chain. An originator of the modern mail-order business, Aaron Montgomery Ward, grew up in Niles. Harry Gordon Selfridge, who established one of the most famous stores in London, England, came from Jackson.

Joseph L. Hudson of Detroit was another important store owner in Michigan. He founded the J.L. Hudson Company, Michigan's largest department store.

FOUR WHEELS AND AN ENGINE

Of all the men who made Michigan famous through the development of the automobile, Henry Ford is probably the most prominent.

Putting the World on Wheels *is a painting of a 1913 Detroit scene.*

Ford had three main ideas that changed the way American industry operated. He created the modern assembly line, where the product moves down a line and each person on the line adds something new to it. He was the first to see that if he made a product that enough people wanted to have and could afford to buy there would be created what we call a "mass market," and he created the first mass market with his Model T car. He was also the first to see that a liberal wage policy for his employees was good business as well as fair labor policy.

In January, 1914, Ford announced that he would pay his workers five dollars for an eight-hour work day. This was such an unbelievably high wage for those days that his competitors felt he probably would go bankrupt. So many workers came to apply for jobs that there were riots on Woodward Avenue, across from the plant.

Instead of going bankrupt the Ford business prospered. The assembly line and other methods of production that he and his associates developed were responsible for the ability of the Ford plant to pay higher wages and still earn a profit. The moving assembly line made it possible to produce one new Ford every six hours in 1914. Almost ten hours were required to produce a new Ford before the assembly lines began.

Mr. Ford hated war, and in 1914 he called a mediation conference in Europe and sent what was called the *Ford Peace Ship*. It sailed from New York with the hope of bringing about peace but with no very clear idea of how this could be done. When the ship returned in 1916, its passengers had talked with many prominent people on both sides of the war and had held many meetings, but peace was as far away as ever.

Many years later, with his son Edsel, Henry Ford established the Ford Foundation. With its many hundreds of millions of dollars, this is the largest of all the foundations. Through his foundation, Mr. Ford's ideas of helping education and culture and of promoting better government and public affairs are still being furthered today, many years after his death.

UNUSUAL ACCOMPLISHMENTS

An accidental gunshot wound on Mackinac Island was the strange beginning of one of the most famous scientific studies of all time. A young trapper, Alexis St. Martin, was severely wounded in the abdomen by the shot, and the wound never healed, although St. Martin recovered and seemed perfectly healthy otherwise.

A physician on the island, Dr. William Beaumont, began to study the opening in St. Martin's stomach. For the first time it was possible to observe the processes of digestion. He became known as "the man with a window in his stomach." Dr. Beaumont's reports on these observations offered great advances in our knowledge of

*This diorama in the Beaumont Memorial in Mackinac
Island State Park shows the wounding of Alexis St. Martin.*

digestive processes and made him world famous. This knowledge
holds good even today, almost 150 years after St. Martin's accident.

St. Martin, who lived an almost normal life in spite of his
difficulties, married, reared a family, and lived to the age of eighty.

Another Michigan man who became famous for an unusual
accomplishment was Charles A. Lindbergh, who was born in
Detroit. When he flew his plane, the *Spirit of St. Louis,* from New
York to Paris in the first solo flight across the Atlantic, it seemed
that the world had never seen such excitement. "The Lone Eagle,"
as Lindbergh came to be called, has been hailed everywhere as one
of the great heroes of all time.

The prominence that Lindberg's flight gave to aviation helped
promote the rapid rise of commercial flying.

Although they are not generally given the credit, Henry and Edsel
Ford, along with William B. Stout, were probably more responsible
for the success of commercial aviation than almost any other
individuals, with the exception of Lindbergh.

The great inventor Thomas A. Edison spent part of his boyhood at Port Huron and invented an electric battery there. One of the world's most influential labor leaders, Walter Reuther, was a Michigan man. He was president of the United Auto Workers for many years. The famous atomic scientist and Nobel Prize winner, Glenn T. Seaborg, comes from Ishpeming.

MICHIGAN WORDS

Many prominent writers, composers, and entertainers have been associated with Michigan. One of the world's most popular poets for many years was Edgar A. Guest of Detroit. His many poems were usually written about everyday situations. Will Carleton set his famous "Over the Hills to the Poorhouse" in Hillsdale. He practiced his well-known lectures on his farm animals, and said that the horses generally went to sleep during the lectures! Hillsdale also contributed to Rose Hartwick Thorpe's "Curfew Shall Not Ring Tonight." The bell written about in this work is the bell that hangs in the Hillsdale village square.

Still another well-loved Michigan writer was Edna Ferber of Kalamazoo. She wrote many famous novels, including *Giant* and *So Big*.

One of the best liked of all Christian hymns, "The Old Rugged Cross," was composed in Albion by Reverend George Bennard, a Methodist minister. At the site of his home, on U.S. Highway 131 near Reed City, there is now a large wooden cross. A three-ton granite cross at Pokagon marks the site where the song was sung for the first time.

Although the poet Henry Wadsworth Longfellow had no personal connection with Michigan, one of his most famous poems, *The Song of Hiawatha,* was associated with Michigan. *Hiawatha* was based on the writings of Henry R. Schoolcraft. On his trip with Governor Lewis Cass in 1820, Schoolcraft had become interested in the Indians and their culture. His wife, Jane Johnston, was part Indian. With her help, Schoolcraft gathered information on the Indians and their lives. Eventually he became one of the greatest American authorities on Indians. He published many books and it was his work that gave Longfellow the background for his writings.

MICHIGAN MUSIC

One of the most unusual and best-known music organizations anywhere is the National Music Camp at Interlochen, founded by Joseph E. Maddy. This is a summer camp-school in a beautiful woodland setting, where talented music students from all over the country come to study with prominent teachers and have an opportunity to play music with other equally talented young people. The idea of teaching music in such an outdoor setting has spread to many other parts of the country and to other nations as well.

The Detroit Symphony Orchestra has achieved wide international fame. Founded in 1914, it came into its own with the selection of Ossip Gabrilowitsch as its permanent conductor. By the beginning of its sixth year, the orchestra had a new building for a permanent home and a regular playing membership of ninety musicians. William H. Murphy and Horace E. Dodge, two prominent Detroit industrialists, each gave $100,000 for the new building, and many other subscriptions also came in to make the building possible.

In more recent years, Michigan—especially Detroit—has become famous for what has come to be known as "the Motown sound." The name "Motown" comes from one of Detroit's most important nicknames, "The Motor City." Two of the entertainers who began their lives and careers in Michigan are Stevie Wonder and Diana Ross. Wonder grew up in Saginaw, began his singing career at age thirteen, and has gone on to become an internationally recognized composer and singer. Ross was born and reared in Detroit, and began her career with a singing group called The Supremes. She has also appeared in motion pictures.

Other prominent entertainers who were born in Michigan include comedians Danny Thomas, Lily Tomlin, and Gilda Radner, actresses Betty Hutton and Ellen Burstyn, and actor Michael Moriarty.

74

Teaching and Learning

The people and government of Michigan have always been strong supporters of good education. Michigan was the first state to provide for a state superintendent of public instruction.

The University of Michigan is considered the first university ever established by any of the states. It is often called "the mother of state universities." It began in Detroit 1817, and its beginnings were aided by the advanced thinking and efforts of such men as Lewis Cass, William Woodbridge, Judge Augustus B. Woodward, Father Gabriel Richard, and Reverend John Monteith. The University moved to Ann Arbor, its present home, in 1837. A gift of land there from the Indians as part of the Treaty of Fort Meigs gave great help and encouragement to the school at an early date in its development.

The first university hospital in the United States was established at the University of Michigan in 1869. It also had the first school of public health in the country. Michigan was also the first major university in this country to admit women. In 1902, the University's football team won the very first Rose Bowl game ever played. Michigan Stadium seats about 105,000 and is the largest college-owned stadium in the United States.

Michigan State University at East Lansing is said to be the oldest institution in the world devoted to teaching scientific agriculture. Its first building was erected in 1857. Today it is the state's largest university and recently became the third Michigan institution to have a school of medicine.

Wayne State University is the largest center of learning in Detroit. Most of its students live in the Detroit area. It has grown rapidly since the 1950s and has many important colleges, including medicine, law, and mortuary science.

Ferris State University in Big Rapids has one of the nation's most important colleges of pharmacy.

Detroit ranks high among major American cities in its library service. The city has twenty-nine branch libraries with a total of more than two million volumes. The University of Michigan alone has nearly four million volumes in its library system.

Enchantment of Michigan

DETROIT

Michigan is one of the most popular states for tourists to visit. Detroit, the oldest major city in the Midwest, has many tourist attractions in its environs.

One of the most interesting things about Detroit is that it is located less than one mile from a foreign country. Many visitors and Detroiters often drive across the Ambassador Bridge or through the Detroit-Windsor Tunnel to visit Windsor, Ontario. The bridge was opened in 1929 and the tunnel a year later. Before that ferries plied the short distance across the Detroit River.

Detroit had been a town for 125 years before it felt the need for a town hall. Today the City-County Building, which was built in 1955, is part of a great new Civic Center, one of the finest of its kind. Also in the Civic Center is the Veterans' Memorial Building, on the site where Antoine de la Mothe Cadillac and his French settlers first landed in 1701.

The Children's Museum, Detroit Institute of Arts, Detroit Historical Museum, Main Library, and the International Institute of Folk Art (which displays exhibits of more than forty ethnic groups) are all located within a few blocks of each other on Woodward Avenue. Wayne State University has its campus in the same area, and all are visited by thousands of people each year.

Detroit's Masonic Temple is just about the largest in the world, and this magnificent building has an entire cathedral within its walls.

The park on Belle Isle in the Detroit River ranks high in beauty and features among American city parks. It offers an aquarium, horticulture building, children's zoo, gardens, riding stables, and many other attractions. The island supposedly took its name from that of Governor Lewis Cass's daughter, Isabella. The English first bought it from the Indians for five barrels of rum, three rolls of tobacco, three pounds (nearly one and one-half kilograms) of red paint, and a belt of wampum. This amounts to about $970, which is still more than another group of Indians received for Manhattan Island.

Sunrise on Lake Superior, Alger County.

The Dossin Great Lakes Museum is located on the south shore of Belle Isle. It tells the great story of ships and sailors on the lakes. There is a fine collection of lake ship models and Great Lakes marine paintings at the museum.

The new Renaissance Center, built in the mid-1970s in Detroit's riverfront Civic Center, contains beautiful tall buildings with a hotel, restaurants, and offices. From the hotel's observation deck there is a panoramic view of Detroit and Windsor, as well as a view of Belle Isle and the many freighters and pleasure craft that sail the Detroit River.

An annual attraction in Detroit is the Michigan State Fair. Established in 1849, it is the oldest of all the state fairs.

Among Detroit's many memorials is a bronze statue of Stevens T. Mason. His body was returned to Michigan from the East in 1905. He had died in the East in a kind of self-imposed exile from his beloved Michigan. Michigan's youngest governor was only thirty-one years old when he died in 1842.

One of the finest residential sections in the country is Grosse Pointe, northeast of Detroit on Lake St. Clair. Grosse Pointe is actually a number of separate towns stretching a few miles along the lake.

Fort Wayne is an appealing attraction for visitors to Detroit. The fort was built in 1846 and named in honor of General "Mad" Anthony Wayne. Fortunately, the fort can still be seen today almost exactly as it was originally constructed. It is considered the best-preserved pre-Civil War fort in the United States. Exhibits inside its buildings tell the story of Detroit's progress from a small fortified trading post to a major city.

HISTORICAL DEARBORN

One of the most frequently visited tourist areas anywhere is Dearborn, where Henry Ford founded so many interesting museums and exhibits. Dearborn is the home of the Henry Ford Museum and Greenfield Village. It is located immediately west of Detroit.

The Greenfield Village clock.

Left: The Martha-Mary Chapel at Greenfield Village. Below: The Stern-wheel paddleboat **Suwanee** *offers rides into the past at Suwanee Park in Greenfield Village.*

Particularly popular at Greenfield Village is the "Street of Early American Shops," showing the work of craftsmen who used hand tools. Visitors can see the work being done in those shops exactly as it was done in the early days. There is a candle shop, wrought-iron shop, toy shop, gun and locksmith shop, millinery shop, and fancy-goods shop. Also in the museum are displays of early autos, historic planes, locomotives, and other mechanical arts.

Visitors who stay at the Dearborn Inn reside for the night in the homes of famous people such as Walt Whitman, Edgar Allan Poe, Barbara Frietchie, and Oliver Wolcott.

Ford considered Greenfield Village his tribute to American men of genius. He gave particular attention to Thomas A. Edison in the Edison Institute and Menlo Park compound.

Ford is generally thought to have considered Edison the greatest American who had ever lived. Edison was also the first prominent person to encourage Ford in his development of the automobile. Edison's laboratory at Menlo Park, New Jersey, has been reproduced with great accuracy. Even the reddish soil around the laboratory has been imported from New Jersey.

Altogether, at Greenfield Village there are more than one hundred historic buildings. These have been moved there from all sections of the country and restored when necessary. They include the birthplace of Ford himself and the bicycle shop of Wilbur and Orville Wright, who built and flew the first airplane at Kitty Hawk, North Carolina. Visitors may ride a horse-drawn carriage, sail on a Mississippi paddlewheel steamer, view an old mill, visit a blacksmith shop, or have a tintype picture taken.

Dearborn is also the location of the Ford Motor Company's Rouge River plant, one of the largest nongovernment plants in the world. Tours through the plant are available.

HOLLAND IN AMERICA

In 1847 a group of Dutch settlers chose a site for a new town in Michigan. They called their little settlement Holland in honor of the country of their birth. In the early years, most of the Dutch settlers who flocked to Holland, Michigan, were escaping from religious persecution.

The Dutch people in Michigan were extremely hardworking and industrious. They dug a canal to connect the town with Lake Michigan and they also built a bridge. Before long the new town was prospering. All through its early years the leader of Holland was its founder, the Reverend Albertus Christiaan Van Raalte.

Today, Holland is a center of thriving businesses and industry. Among other factories, it has the only wooden-shoe manufacturing plant in this country.

Holland is also the home of one of the best and most famous annual festivals in the country. This is the annual Tulip Festival. For Festival time in May the residents wear Dutch costumes and wooden shoes. There are floral parades, pageants, and tulips everywhere. Great crowds are always attracted to Holland for the event.

SOUTHERN MICHIGAN

Several southern Michigan cities have unusual names. Two pioneer settlers in one of these towns both had wives named Ann.

The Nellis tulip farm near Holland Michigan.

These women liked to sit under their grape arbor so much that their husbands named the town Ann Arbor, which today is the celebrated home of the University of Michigan. Among the principal points of interest there are the grounds, buildings, and museums of the University.

In its Indian form, the name *kalamazoo* means "where the water boils in the pot." The city of Kalamazoo was the first in the United States to build a permanent mall. This was done by taking all vehicles off the principal shopping street and turning it into a beautiful parklike area. Since Kalamazoo pioneered this plan, a number of other cities across the country have created similar malls.

When an early land surveyor and an Indian had a fight on the banks of a creek in 1825 they could hardly have known that their "battle" was going to give its name to the city of Battle Creek. Among the many attractions of Battle Creek, the Leila Aboretum is said to be one of the finest in the world. The W.K. Kellogg Bird Sanctuary on Wintergreen Lake near Battle Creek is the largest of its kind in the country.

Visitors to the region of Bloomfield Hills may well be surprised by the music which seems to float through the air. They are listening to the world's second-largest carillon, installed in 1960 at the Kirk-in-the-Hills Presbyterian Church. There are seventy-seven bells, weighing a total of sixty-six tons (nearly sixty metric tons).

Nearby Adrian is known as the "Maple City of Michigan." It was the terminal of the first railroad built west of New York State and connected Adrian with Toledo, 30 miles (about 48 kilometers) away.

In Lansing, the capitol building is made of sandstone. It has a rotunda paved with glass blocks set into an iron framework to form the floor. From the rotunda floor, the visitor can look up to the top of the dome, 175 feet (more than 53 meters) above. There is a grand staircase on either side of the rotunda. One hundred and twenty-three battered, bullet-torn flags are displayed in cases around the rotunda. These are the Civil War battle flags of Michigan.

When the capitol was dedicated in 1879, it was very much in advance of its time. Gas lights were instantly lit by electric switches. There was a steam-operated elevator.

The second-largest collection of fingerprints in the United States is on file at the Michigan State Police Headquarters in East Lansing. Only the Federal Bureau of Investigation (FBI) file in Washington is larger, but the FBI file was established later. In fact, Michigan's file was the model for the one in Washington.

Near Lansing, in Eaton Rapids, is the national headquarters of the Veterans of Foreign Wars. This is a city in itself on a 640-acre (259-hectare) site and serves as the home for several hundred widows and orphans of veterans.

One of Michigan's most unusual organizations is the House of David, a religious group founded in 1903 in Benton Harbor by Benjamin Purnell. This group is particularly remembered for its famous long-bearded baseball team.

Grand Rapids is Michigan's second-largest city. The Grand Rapids Public Museum has a large furniture collection, the only one of its kind. Gerald R. Ford, the thirty-eighth president of the United States, was reared in Grand Rapids.

Jackson is noted for a beautiful fountain with illuminated cascades of water. A much grimmer landmark of Jackson is the State Prison of Southern Michigan, one of the world's largest walled prisons.

The courthouse of Lapeer County is the oldest in the state. It was built in 1839.

Frankenmuth is noted for its Church Bells in the Forest and its year-round display of Christmas decorations.

Across the state, in Muskegon, is the grave of Jonathan Walker, who was the "man with the branded hand" in the writings of the poet John Greenleaf Whittier. Charles Hackley, who made his fortune in the lumber business, contributed a large sum of money to make possible the fine art museum in Muskegon.

IN THE NORTHERN TIER

Chesaning, not far from Saginaw, is proud to entertain visitors on its lovely showboat. The mysterious sinkholes of Alpena are another inviting attraction of the northeastern part of the state.

The site of Ludington is remembered as the place where the famous explorer-priest Jacques Marquette died in 1675. Father Marquette had been pushing on to reach the mission he had established at St. Ignace. There he could be treated for his serious illness, but his brave heart gave out and his companions buried him near the spot where he died.

Father Marquette's body was moved two years after his death to St. Ignace. The town where he died was first called Marquette, but the name was later changed to the name of its founder, James Ludington.

Of course, at the time of Father Marquette's death there was no town there, but at the place where his death occurred is a memorial cross, and the river that empties into Lake Michigan nearby is called the Pere Marquette in his memory.

On the Au Sable River in Iosco County is the Lumberman's Memorial, a monument to the many people who have worked in Michigan's lumber industry.

Houghton Lake, source of the Muskegon River, is the largest lake wholly inside the boundaries of Michigan.

A unique memorial is the one one found in Kewadin in Antrim County. This is a cairn built of stones from every one of Michigan's eighty-three counties. It was built in memory of Hugh J. Gray, the person who began organized tourist promotion in the state.

Frankfort has gained an international reputation as a glider-soaring site. Because the winds and other conditions there seem to be just right, many world records in gliding have been set there.

Although not many Indians remain in Michigan, the Ottawa Indians still maintain their tribal capital at Harbor Springs and hold their ceremonial assemblies there each year.

One of the great opera houses of the world was built at Manistee by lumber king T.J. Ramsdell around the turn of the last century. It was one of the largest of its time and still has one of the greatest stages anywhere. It is used now as a summer theater. The salt brine found at Manistee has been noted for its use in health bath immersion treatments. The name *manistee* in the local Indian language has the romantic translation of "spirit of the woods."

84

One of the Indian legends collected by Henry R. Schoolcraft tells of the mother bear and her two cubs who started to swim across Lake Michigan to look for food. Just before they reached the shore the two cubs sank. The mother bear crawled up on the shore and lay down on the bank where she could look out over the spot where her cubs drowned. Before long the shifting sands covered her. Today, the story goes, that mother bear has become Sleeping Bear sand dune, and two small islands off the shore are the bear cubs.

Another island with many memories is Beaver Island. Twenty buildings of the Mormon period have been preserved, and the home of James Jesse Strang, who set himself up as a king, is now open to visitors as a museum. Also on the island is the grave of Dr. Fedore Protar, a Russian count exiled by the Czar in the nineteenth century for freeing his serfs. Dr. Protar attended the residents of the island without ever charging them a fee.

The world's longest toboggan run at Grayling sweeps tobogganists down its 3,000-foot (over 900-meter) length at speeds up to 100 miles (161 kilometers) per hour.

Near Traverse City, at the tip of Old Mission Peninsula, is Michigan's westernmost point on an imaginary line exactly halfway between the equator and the North Pole. The line is marked in many places across the state. Traverse City itself is famous for its annual cherry festival.

On Burt Lake, near Indian River, is the Indian River Shrine. A cross 31 feet (9.45 meters) high bears one of the largest figures ever made to represent Christ. It was created by the well-known sculptor Marshall Fredericks.

The area around Mackinaw City is one of the most interesting in the state. "Big Mac," as the Mackinac Bridge is familiarly known, is one of the world's great tourist attractions in its own right, as well as being a tremendous help to traffic entering or leaving the Upper Peninsula. Almost in the shadow of Big Mac is old Fort Michilimackinac. Restoration of the fort, begun in 1959, is still going on.

Few areas in the United States have been the scene of more dramatic and historic events than Mackinac Island. The name is thought to mean "great turtle" because of the island's shape.

Fort Michilimackinac in the shadow of
"Big Mac," the Mackinac bridge.

The island is located at the crossroads of a very large territory. This strategic location, between the Upper and Lower peninsulas and between Lakes Huron and Michigan, made it important in military maneuvers and in settlement. Mackinac Island had a long and important history even before Detroit was founded.

Today, in addition to being a pleasant summer resort, with the largest summer hotel in the world, the island has kept alive its historic memories for its visitors. The effect of the past is strengthened by the fact that no automobiles are allowed on the island. Vehicles are limited to carriages or bicycles.

On its high bluff overlooking the harbor, Old Fort Mackinac stands guard. Built in 1780, it is preserved as nearly as possible just as it looked then. Scattered about the island are many natural scenic wonders, such as Arch Rock. Mackinac Island is the only place where the sun can be seen to rise over one Great Lake and set in another.

Strangely, Mackinac Island had been named a national park in 1875, but was turned over to Michigan in 1895 and became Michigan's first state park.

86

THE UPPER PENINSULA

There still is one national park within Michigan's boundaries. That is wonderful Isle Royale National Park, where there are no roads or wheeled vehicles. The whole area remains almost completely unchanged by man. The nearest mainland is 22 miles (35.4 kilometers) away from this island, the largest in Lake Superior. It is 45 miles (72.4 kilometers) long, five to eight miles (8 to 13 kilometers) wide, and is surrounded by more than 200 smaller islands.

On Isle Royale is one of the largest remaining herds of great antlered moose in the United States. They are thought to have crossed over to the island on the ice in the severe winter of 1912. When the ice melted they could no longer get back to the mainland.

A great tourist center of the Upper Peninsula is the region of the St. Marys River, centered at Sault Ste. Marie. In this oldest of all the cities in Michigan, there is a Chippewa museum containing many relics of precolonial times. The museum is housed in the historic building where Henry Schoolcraft wrote his *Indian Tales,* from which Longfellow wrote *The Song of Hiawatha.*

In Sault Ste. Marie, visitors may also see a model of the city, river, canal, and locks as they looked in the mid-1850s when the first locks and canal were new.

Sault Ste. Marie is the only gateway between Canada and the United States on a 300-mile (483-kilometer) stretch of the border. The next gateway west is in far northeastern Minnesota, and Port Huron, Michigan, is the next gateway in the other direction.

Skiing in the Upper Peninsula is world renowned. Ski jumping in the United States had its beginning at Ishpeming in 1887. Today the National Ski Museum and the National Ski Hall of Fame are there.

Porcupine Mountains State Park in Ontonagon County is the largest recreational state park in the nation. It covers 58,000 acres (about 23,500 hectares). Another popular Upper Peninsula state park is Fort Wilkins State Park at Copper Harbor. Its old stockade has been restored and maintained as a frontier post.

This combination of the old and the new provides one of Michigan's attractions as a tourist state.

Instant Facts

Became the 26th state, January 26, 1837
Capital—Lansing, founded 1847
State motto—*Si Quaeris Peninsulam Amoenam, Circumspice* (If You Seek a Pleasant
       Peninsula, Look Around You)
State nicknames—The Wolverine State, Water Wonderland
State bird—Robin
State fish—Trout
State tree—White Pine
State flower—Apple Blossom
State song (unofficial)—"Michigan, My Michigan"
Area—96,791 square miles (250,688 square kilometers) including water area;
       57,022 square miles (147,686 square kilometers), land area only
Greatest length (north to south)—215 miles (346 kilometers), Upper Peninsula;
       286 miles (460 kilometers), Lower Peninsula
Greatest width (east to west)—334 miles (538 kilometers), Upper Peninsula;
       200 miles (322 kilometers), Lower Peninsula
Highest point—1,980 feet (603.5 meters), Mt. Curwood
Lowest point—572 feet (174.35 meters)
Geographic center—Wetford, 5 miles (8 kilometers) north northwest of Cadillac
Highest recorded temperature—112° F. (44.4° C.), Mio
Lowest recorded temperature—-51° F. (-46° C.), Vanderbilt
Population—1980 census: 9,262,070 (1985 estimate: 9,088,000)
Population density—158 persons per square mile (61 per square kilometer), 1980
       census
Rank in density—8th
Number of counties—83

Major Cities	1980 Census	1984 Estimate
Detroit	1,203,339	1,089,000
Grand Rapids	181,843	183,000
Warren	161,134	no estimate
Flint	159,611	149,000
Lansing	130,414	128,000
Sterling Heights	108,999	no estimate
Ann Arbor	107,969	107,700
Livonia	104,814	no estimate
Dearborn	90,660	87,000

You Have a Date with History

1618-1622—Etienne Brulé and Grenoble become first Europeans in
       Michigan
c. 1634—Jean Nicolet passes through Straits of Mackinac

88

1641—Fathers Isaac Jogues and Charles Raymbault reach Sault de Sainte Marie

1668—Fathers Jacques Marquette and Claude Dablon found first permanent European settlement

1669—Adrien Jolliet becomes first European in Lower Peninsula

1671—François Daumont claims interior of continent for French in Pageant of the Sault, June 14

1673—Marquette and Jolliet leave St. Ignace on exploration

1675—Marquette dies near present-day Ludington

1679—La Salle builds first French fort in lower Michigan; *Griffon* vanishes

1686—Daniel Greysolon builds Fort St. Joseph at present-day Port Huron

1701—Antoine de la Mothe Cadillac founds Detroit

1711—Cadillac forced to leave Detroit

1715—Fort Michilimackinac founded

1760—French rule in Detroit ends

1763—Pontiac siege begins at Detroit

1781—Spanish flag in Michigan

1783—Treaty of Paris settles American Revolution, gives Michigan to Americans

1787—Northwest Territory established by Northwest Ordinance

1796—British evacuate Detroit

1800—Michigan becomes part of Indiana Territory

1802—Detroit incorporated as a city

1805—Michigan Territory created, Detroit is capital

1808—John Jacob Astor founds American Fur Company at Mackinac Islands

1809—First book printed in Michigan

1812—Detroit surrenders to British in War of 1812

1813—Detroit recaptured by Americans; Lewis Cass becomes governor of Michigan, October

1815—Pacification Dinner, Detroit, March 29

1817—University of Michigan founded in Detroit

1818—First steamboat visits Detroit; Michigan Territory enlarged

1828—Territorial capitol built at Detroit

1831—Stevens T. Mason becomes governor

1832—Father Gabriel Richard dies, September 13

1833—Chief Black Hawk visits Detroit, July 4

1835—Michigan gives Toledo area to Ohio, receives Upper Peninsula

1837—Michigan becomes 26th state, January; University of Michigan opens at Ann Arbor

1840—Copper discovered in Upper Peninsula

1842—Stevens T. Mason dies

1844—Iron ore discovered at Negaunee

1846—Mormons settle Beaver Island

1847—Lansing becomes capital

1848—Legislature meets for first time at Lansing

1854—Republican Party organized, Jackson, July 6
1855—Sault Ste. Marie ship canal opens
1857—Michigan State University opens
1871—Forest fires, October 8
1879—State Capitol dedicated, Lansing
1884-1885—First self-propelled vehicle in Michigan
1887—R.E. Olds builds 3-wheel steam car, Lansing
1896—First automobile in Detroit
1908—First Model T Ford built
1914—Detroit Symphony Orchestra founded
1920—WWJ makes first radio news broadcast, Detroit, August 31
1929—Ambassador Bridge opens
1930—Detroit-Windsor Tunnel opens
1935—United Automobile Workers organized
1957—Mackinac Bridge opens
1959—St. Lawrence Seaway opens
1974—Gerald R. Ford of Grand Rapids becomes 38th president of the
        United States
1984—Detroit Tigers win World Series

Thinkers, Doers, Fighters

People of renown who have been associated with Michigan

Baraja, Father Frederic
Beaumont, Dr. William
Bunche, Ralph J.
Cadillac, Antoine de la Mothe
Cass, Lewis
Cavelier, Robert (Sieur de la Salle)
Chrysler, Walter P.
Custer, George Armstrong
Daumont, Francois (Sieur de
   St. Lusson)
Dow, Herbert H.
Ford, Edsel
Ford, Henry I
Gabrilowitsch, Ossip
Gray, Hugh J.
Guest, Edgar A.
Haldane, William
Harvey, Charles T.
Houghton, Douglass
Hudson, J.L.
Hutton, Betty
Jolliet, Adrian

Jolliet, Louis
Kellogg, Will Keith
King, Charles G.
Kresge, Sebastian S.
Lindbergh, Charles A.
Marquette, Father Jacques
Mason, Steven T.
Monteith, John
Nicolet, Jean
Olds, Ransom E.
Post, C.W.
Richard, Father Gabriel
Romney, George W.
Ross, Diana
Stout, William B.
Schoolcraft, Henry R.
Thomas, Danny
Tomlin, Lily
Van Raalte, Rev. Albertus
   Christiaan
Wonder, Stevie
Woodward, Augustus

Annual Events

January—Tipuptown Festival (Ice Fishing) Houton Lake
February—Winter Carnival, Alpena
February—Ice Revue, Escanaba
May—National Mushroom Contest, Boyne City
May—Blossom Festival, Blessing of the Blossoms, Benton Harbor
May—Tulip Festival, Holland
June—Lilac Festival, Mackinac Island
July—Sailing Races, to Mackinac Island
July—Top O' Michigan Marathon, outboard races, Cheboygan
August—Potato Festival, Munger
September—Walking Races, International Walkers Association, across
  Mackinac Bridge (Labor Day)
September—Archery Festival, Lewiston
October—Red Flannel Festival, Cedar Springs
October—Women's National Bear Hunt, Kalkaska
October—National Automobile Show, Detroit
November—Santa Claus Parade, Detroit

Governors of the State of Michigan

Steven T. Mason, 1835-1840
William Woodbridge, 1840-1841
James Wright Gordon, 1841
John S. Barry, 1842-1846
Alpheus Felch, 1846-1847
William L. Greenly, 1847
Epaphroditus Ransom, 1848-1850
John S. Barry, 1850-1851
Robert McClelland, 1852-1853
Andrew Parsons, 1853-1854
Kingsley S. Bingham, 1855-1858
Moses Wisner, 1859-1860
Austin Blair, 1861-1864
Henry H. Crapo, 1865-1868
Henry P. Baldwin, 1869-1872
John J. Bagley, 1873-1876
Charles M. Croswell, 1877-1880
David H. Jerome, 1881-1882
Josiah W. Begole, 1883-1884
Russell A. Alger, 1885-1886
Cyrus G. Luce, 1887-1890
Edwin B. Winans, 1891-1892

John T. Rich, 1893-1896
Hazen S. Pingree, 1897-1900
Aaron T. Bliss, 1901-1904
Fred M. Warner, 1905-1910
Chase S. Osborn, 1911-1912
Woodbridge N. Ferris, 1913-1916
Albert E. Sleeper, 1917-1920
Alexander J. Groesbeck, 1921-1926
Fred W. Green, 1927-1930
Wilber M. Brucker, 1931-1932
William A. Comstock, 1933-1934
Frank D. Fitzgerald, 1935-1936
Frank Murphy, 1937-1938
Frank D. Fitzgerald, 1939
Luren D. Dickinson, 1939-1940
Murray D. Van Wagoner, 1941-1942
Harry F. Kelly, 1943-1946
Kim Sigler, 1947-1948
G. Mennen Williams, 1949-1960
John B. Swainson, 1961-1963
George W. Romney, 1963-1969
William G. Milliken, 1969-1983
James J. Blanchard, 1983-

Index

94

PICTURE CREDITS

Color photographs courtesy of the following: Travel Bureau, Michigan Department of Commerce, pages 13, 36, 43, 44, 64, 76, 79 (top); © Michigan Bell Telephone Company, Robert Thom, 8, 18, 27, 32, 35, 39, 70; News Department, Ford Motor Company, 62; Ford Motor Company, 58, 59, 61; Greenfield Village and Henry Ford Museum, 40, 66, 79 (middle), 79 (bottom); The Exhibit Museum, Alexander G. Ruthven Museums, The University of Michigan, 14 (bottom), 46, 50; Michigan Department of Natural Resources, Mackinac Island State Park, 21, 72; William L. Clements Library, University of Michigan, 25; Stokes Collection, New York Public Library, 30; Architect of the U.S. Capitol 20; USDA, Soil Conservation Service photo by Erwin W. Cole, 49, U.S. Department of Agriculture, Robert Hailstock, Jr., 52.

Illustrations on back cover by Len W. Meents.

ABOUT THE AUTHOR

With the publication of his first book for school use when he was twenty, **Allan Carpenter** began a career as an author that has spanned more than 135 books. After teaching in the public schools of Des Moines, Mr. Carpenter began his career as an educational publisher at the age of twenty-one when he founded the magazine *Teachers Digest.* In the field of educational periodicals, he was responsible for many innovations. During his many years in publishing, he has perfected a highly organized approach to handling large volumes of factual material: after extensive traveling and having collected all possible materials, he systematically reviews and organizes everything. From his apartment high in Chicago's John Hancock Building, Allan recalls, "My collection and assimilation of materials on the states and countries began before the publication of my first book." Allan is the founder of Carpenter Publishing House and of Infordata International, Inc., publishers of *Issues in Education* and *Index to U. S. Government Periodicals.* When he is not writing or traveling, his principal avocation is music. He has been the principal bassist of many symphonies, and he managed the country's leading non-professional symphony for twenty-five years.